Decorative PAPERCUTTING

25 BEAUTIFUL PAPER PROJECTS TO MAKE

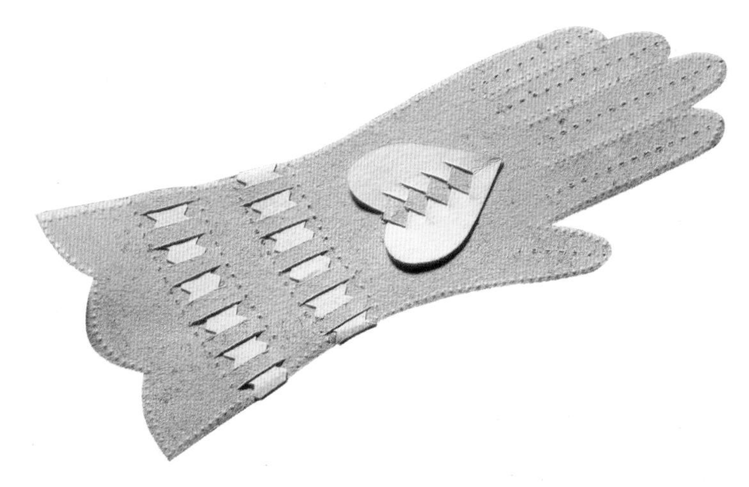

DEBORAH SCHNEEBELI-MORRELL

COLLINS & BROWN

To the memory of Malgorzata Spurring Swiantk

First published in Great Britain in 1998
by Collins & Brown Limited
London House
Great Eastern Wharf
Parkgate Road
London SW11 4NQ

1 3 5 7 9 8 6 4 2

British Library Cataloguing-in-Publication Data:
A catalogue record for this book is available from the British Library.

ISBN 1 85585 6204 (hardback edition)

ISBN 1 85585 653 0 (paperback edition)

Conceived, edited and designed by Collins & Brown Limited

Editor: Gillian Haslam
Designer: Sara Kidd
Photographer: Heini Schneebeli
Stylist: Deborah Schneebeli-Morrell

Reproduction by Hong Kong Graphic and Printing Ltd.

Printed and bound in Hong Kong by Dai Nippon Printing Co. (HK) Ltd.

AUTHOR'S ACKNOWLEDGEMENTS
Very special thanks to Heini Schneebeli for his care and attention to detail in taking the wonderful photographs in this book. I would also like to thank Graham Day for his help with the project on page 117, and my friend Catherine Fried for her help and encouragement. A big thank you to Gillian Haslam for her excellent editing and continuous support, to Sara Kidd for her design and special thanks to Cindy Richards and Kate Haxell at Collins & Brown.

My gratitude extends to all the unknown peasant artists whose work constantly serves as an inspiration to me.

Contents

Introduction

THE UNIVERSAL ART OF papercutting is a well-known, traditional folk craft. Examples appear throughout history and in many disparate cultures. This truly peasant art form is particularly prevalent in central Europe and central and north America. Poland has a long history of this craft, brightly coloured examples are used to decorate rural homes, and even stables. A number of projects in the book, such as the crepe paper girandole on page 10 and the urn of roses on page 18 have been directly inspired by this Polish tradition.

Swiss papercutting is perhaps more detailed and refined. In the mountain regions it was traditionally the men who cut intricate, symmetrical designs from folded paper, usually black, to depict village and rural life. The accuracy with which animals, trees and people are cut with small pointed scissors is quite astounding and can only come from a deep knowledge and an endless observation of daily life. The circular pinpricked papercut on page 54 and the Valentine picture on page 70 have been influenced by Swiss traditions.

The early settlers from Europe took the craft of papercutting to North America. The gloved hand gift tags on page 106 take their inspiration from American folk art. The Shaker communities in North America produced beautiful pieces of work by pinpricking a design through cut paper; this technique produces a delicate and extremely intricate pattern.

Papercutting was also popular in England and France in the seventeenth, eighteenth and nineteenth centuries and was widely practised by women as a drawing room skill. Beautiful examples still survive in the form of silhouettes.

Mexico is yet another culture where exquisite examples of papercutting are still made today. Most famous are the festive banners (page 82) made from brightly coloured tissue paper They are strung across ceilings in houses and churches or even outside, and serve as decorations for celebratory events such as weddings, christenings, saints' days and, most famous of all, The Day of the Dead festival in early November.

Interest in paper and all its applied techniques of transformation is universal. As a medium it appeals to the most talented, knowledgeable and creative as well as to those with much enthusiasm but little technical ability. The appeal of papercutting is that it is truly inexpensive and the tools and specialist techniques are kept to a minimum. Recycling is an important element - finding, collecting and using small scraps of discarded paper to incorporate into an enduring picture is a magical and rewarding process.

The papers used in this book are very varied in colour, texture, weight and size. They have all been obtained from arts and crafts shops and because they originate from many different countries it is impossible to give standard sizes. Always buy paper in sheets, not in drawing books or as writing paper unless stipulated. You will find that the available sheet size will be more than large enough to create your chosen project. If you are unsure about a paper size, enlarge the template in the book to the required size and check that it fits on the paper sheet. As a rule the weight and texture of the paper is more important than its size.

This Valentine picture, made from scraps of paper, is inspired by Swiss papercutting traditions.

Room Decorations

It is not necessary to use complicated paint finishes to transform your home. Spectacular results can be obtained using the simple art of papercutting. Paper is inexpensive and easily available, so the techniques have long appealed to peasant artists.

Girandole

A GIRANDOLE IS A KIND of folk art chandelier (but without candles!), used to decorate Polish peasant houses. In the inventive way of all folk art, they were made from readily available materials of local origin such as straw, feathers, beans, peas, woollen yarn, frayed paper and brightly coloured tissue paper. Some of the more elaborate spider girandoles were made in the form of complex structures, using the threaded straw as the interconnecting struts. They were often crystalline in shape and composed of many open prisms. Suspended from the low ceilings between long garlands of paperchains, they must have created an atmosphere of richness way beyond the inhabitants' means.

Although the version here is authentic in its style and construction, it is relatively simple to make. When you have mastered the technique you may be inspired enough to make a more elaborate version. It would make an ideal decoration to suspend over a festive table, perhaps a wedding celebration or a Christmas feast.

MATERIALS

Galvanized wire 1.5 mm (1/16 in) thick

Duotone crepe paper in pink, purple, orange, yellow, red, etc

Scissors

White glue

Normal crepe paper in lilac, purple, pink, yellow and orange

Templates (see below)

Pinking shears

Coloured plastic straws

Needle with large eye

Strong thread

Small beads

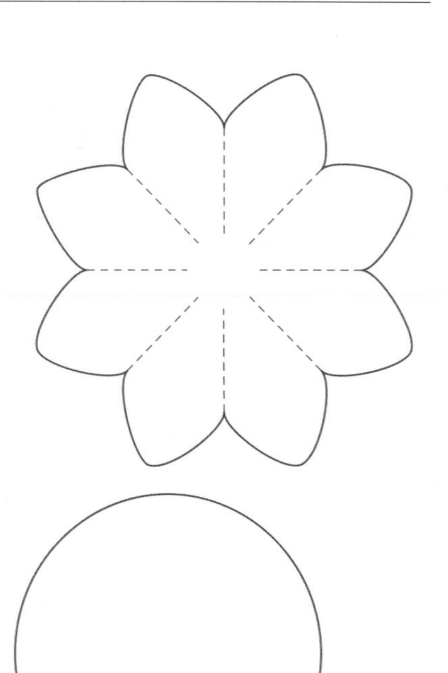

Enlarge these templates on a photocopier to 225%

1

Twist the wire into a ring which measures 30 cm (12 in) in diameter. Cut a strip of the pink/red duotone crepe paper 3 cm (1¼ in) wide from one end of the flattened roll, Make a series of snips 2 cm (¾ in) deep along one side.

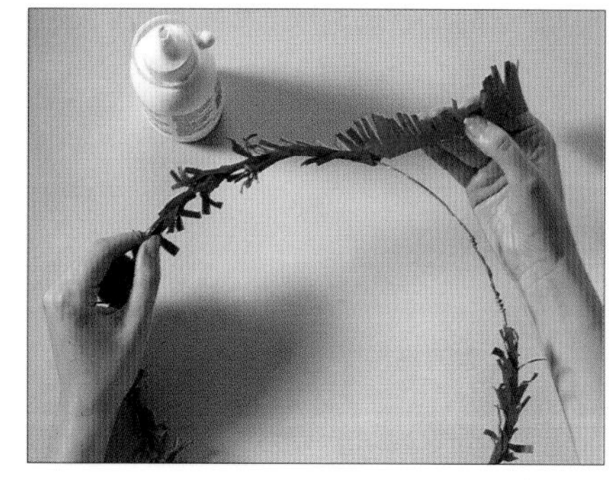

2

Secure one end onto the wire ring with the glue and tightly wind the frilly strip around the wire ring with the pink side facing inwards. Wrap the paper towards you, with the unsnipped edge facing you, so that the frills show. When the two ends meet, glue in place.

6

Cut a 60 cm (24 in) length of the strong thread, thread it through the needle and tie a knot in one end, slip one of the beads on to the end and start to thread alternate layers of the deep and lighter orange snipped discs. Stop when you have completed one pile of each colour.

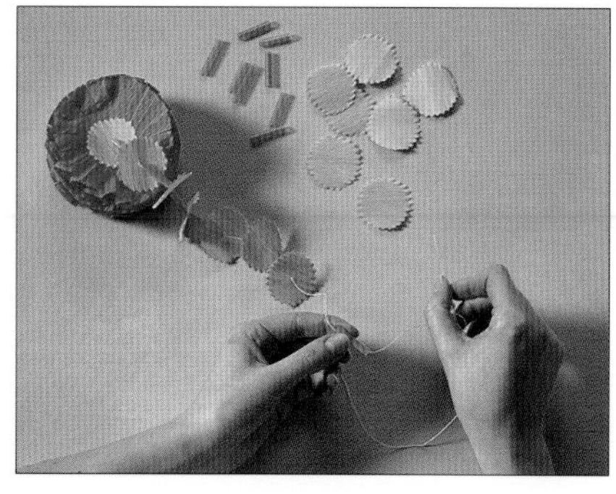

7

Dab glue in the centre of the top orange circle and thread a duotone yellow disc onto the thread. Push down so it sticks to the pom-pom, holding it together. Now thread 15 pink straws and yellow discs. Make another similar pom-pom, then make a matching pair from the two yellows with orange duotone discs and straws. The purple and pink pom-poms are threaded with pale yellow discs and yellow straws.

3

To make the flower which is suspended inside the girandole, place the flower-shaped template on a section cut from the ends of the lilac and the purple normal crepe paper and cut out directly with the scissors. Cut slits between the petals as indicated by the dotted line on the template. Make a fold on each individual petal by pressing firmly between finger and thumb and set aside until step 9.

4

Using the large round template, from the flattened ends of normal crepe paper cut two piles each of pale and dark yellow, two each of light and dark orange and two each of deep purple and bright pink. Snip around the edge as shown. Using the small template and pinking shears, cut 30 each of duotone orange, yellow and pale pink. Cut 15 similar ones from bright pink for the central 'stem'.

5

Cut 30 3 cm (1¼ in) lengths from each of the pink, orange and yellow plastic straws. Cut another 15 orange ones to thread onto the central 'stem'.

8

To attach the pom-pom string to the wire circle, wind the thread around the circle after so that four discs are hanging below it. Attach two of the same colour opposite each other, then suspend the developing girandole from a point above so you can add each new pom-pom evenly. Suspend matching colours directly opposite each other.

9

Make the central pom-pom from lilac and purple petals in the same way and thread with orange straws and pink duotone paper. Suspend this in the centre. Gather the threads together at the top and add another pom-pom made from purple and pink paper. You may need to thread the threads into a larger needle. Dab glue onto the seven threads to stick them together and make into a hanging loop.

Crepe Paper Roses

ONE OF THE MOST traditional techniques of making flowers is the one shown here, using crepe paper. This project uses the brightest colours, but it is worth experimenting with a paler, more subtle range.

To make the rosebuds, take a continuous length of paper and roll the entire length along one side. Wind it tightly, gathering and pinching as you wrap it around the wire. Add the sepals and bind the stem. Larger blooms are made similarly, using a longer length of paper and attaching it to the wire a little more loosely. The sepals can be rolled and turned back to create variety.

The catkins are made by cutting a length of paper 2.5 cm (1 in) wide and approximately 120 cm (48 in) long. Using a needle and matching thread, sew a running stitch along the middle of the strip. Pull the thread to gather the strip tightly and then glue it to the wire, binding the end and the stem in the same way as for the roses. To finish, hold one end of the gathered paper and twist clockwise in a spiral fashion to create the catkin effect.

MATERIALS

Selection of Duotone crepe paper in various colours for the petals and green for the sepals and stems

Scissors

Templates (see page 16)

Paper clips

Tapered chopstick

Soft wire 2 mm (1/8 in) thick, 30 cm (12 in) long for each rose (copper wire is ideal as it bends easily)

White glue

Sepal

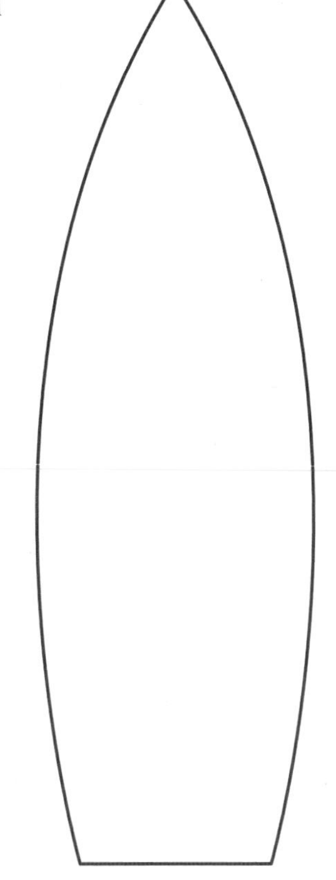

Petal

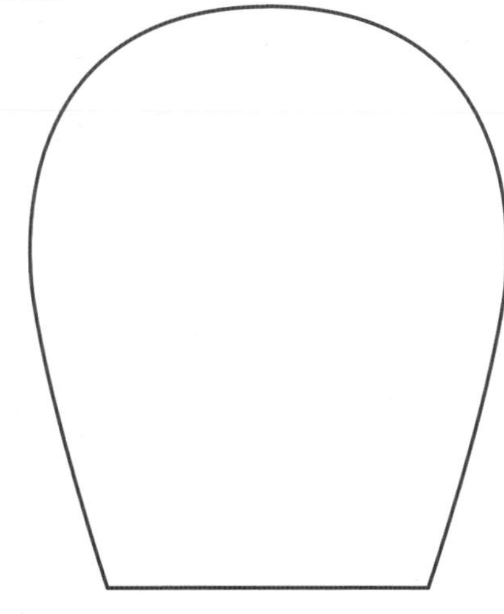

Enlarge these templates on a photocopier 124%

1

Cut a strip of the crepe paper for the petals 10 x 80 cm (4 x 30 in). It is important that the grain of the paper runs along the short edge. Fold the paper concertina-style to give ten layers each 8 cm (3 in) wide. Lay the petal template on top and secure with paper clips. Cut carefully around the template with the scissors.

2

Take three of the petal shapes and using both thumbs, push into the centre of the darker side, creating a three-dimensional effect. Using the tapered chopstick, roll both sides of the top of the petal back over the stick, causing the darker side to curl over to the lighter side. Do the same with the other petals, but roll the light side over to the dark side.

4

Add the seven remaining petals in the same way, placing them with the lighter side facing inwards. Pinch and gather them into place at the bottom. When all the petals are attached, pinch the base of the flower firmly to make sure they are all securely in place on the wire.

5

Using the sepal template, cut out five pieces from the green crepe paper, with the grain running the length of the sepal. Once again, use your thumbs to push in the centre of the sepal to create the shaped effect. Roll one side of the tip over the chopstick so the sepals look as if they have unfurled from the bud.

3

Turn over the end of the wire to form a small loop and dip into the glue. Take one of the three petals with the darker inner side and wrap it around the end of the wire. Add the two remaining darker petals by dabbing a drop of glue at their bases and wrapping them around the first petal to form the deeper coloured centre of the rose.

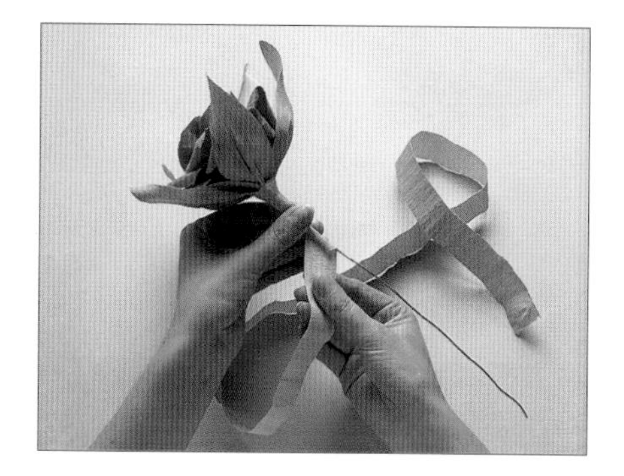

6

Attach the sepals to the rose in the same way as the petals, with the light side facing inwards and a little glue at the base. Pinch to secure. Cut a long strip of green crepe paper 2 cm (¾ in) wide to bind the stem. Add some glue to the base of the flower and with the dark side facing outwards wrap the strip tightly around the base of the flower and down the stem. Smear a little glue along the inside of the strip as you wind it to ensure it does not slip or unravel.

Urn of Roses

A LOVE OF BRIGHT COLOURS and intricate decoration are common to folk culture throughout the world, and have probably developed as an inventive way to compensate for a lack of material richness in peasant life. The making of paper flowers is a typical example of this.

In Poland, formal and symmetrical arrangements such as the project shown here were made and placed in decorative flowerpots or simple vases and used to adorn a home altar, usually positioned on either side of a religious picture or icon. In Mexico, paper marigolds are used to decorate the graves of departed relatives during the famous festival of The Day of the Dead. This is to encourage the presence of humming birds, which are believed to symbolize the souls of the dead. It is thought they are attracted by the 'nectar' of the flowers. In many other parts of the world, most notably India, Thailand and the South Sea islands, honoured guests are graciously adorned with garlands of natural and paper flowers.

This project uses crepe paper which is available in a wide range of bright colours, including the two-tone variety used here. This is formed of two complementary shades of crepe paper glued together, forming a double-sided sheet. It is wonderfully versatile and can be stretched and rolled to produce a three-dimensional effect, making it the ideal material to imitate the various forms of flowers.

MATERIALS

Ready-made flowers, buds and catkins (see page 14)

Wooden dowel 1.5 x 50 cm (¾ x 30 in)

White glue and brush

Wooden block 9 cm (4 in) square x 15 cm (6 in) deep

Drill

Green, purple/mauve and royal blue Duotone crepe paper

Template (see page 21)

Card of a medium thickness

Small scissors

Pinking shears

1

If you are right-handed, hold the dowel in your left hand and begin to wind the stem of the first flower very firmly around it 18 cm (7 in) from one end. (If left-handed, reverse the instructions.) The front of the flower should stand out about 20 cm (8 in) from the dowel.

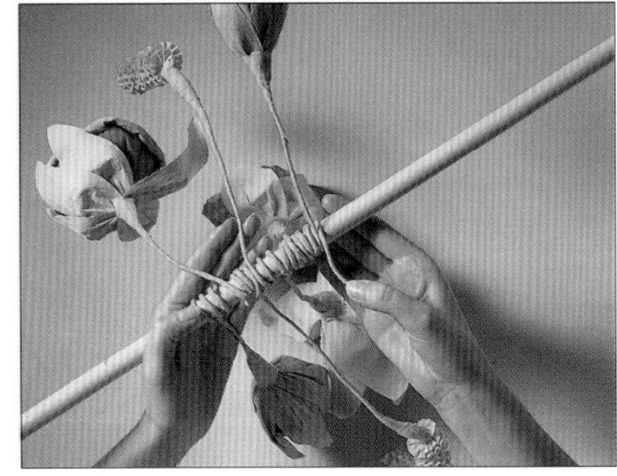

2

Continue to wind the flowers around the dowel in this way, alternating the larger flowers, buds and catkins. It is a good idea to look at the main picture and follow the design shown there.

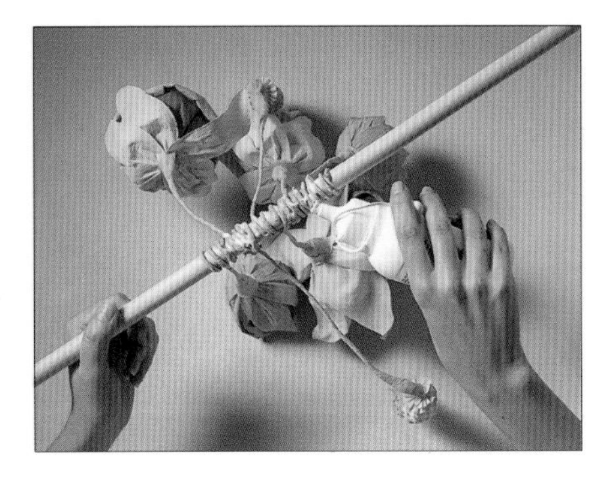

3

As you wind the flowers up the dowel add some white glue to secure them in place. You may like to use a brush to spread the glue so it reaches the front as well as the back. Allow about 30 minutes for the glue to dry so the flowers are held securely in place.

7

Use the template to cut out the urn shape from the card. Cover the card lightly with the glue and press onto the crepe paper. Smooth your hand over the card to make sure the crepe paper sticks evenly.

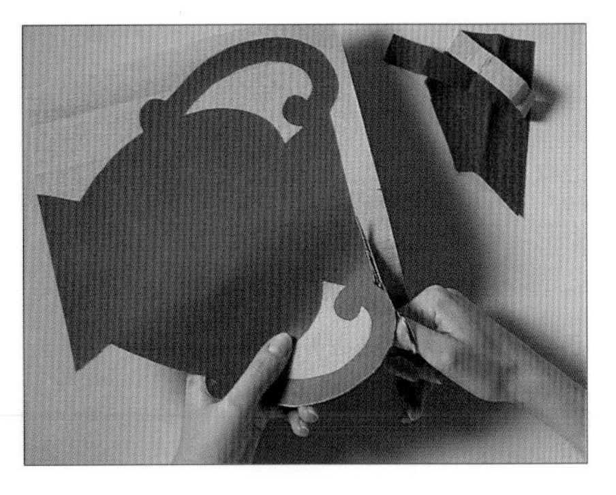

8

Turn the urn over and and cut around the card very carefully with the small scissors. Pay particular attention when cutting inside the two curved handles.

9

Using the pinking shears, cut the purple duotone paper into strips and use both sides (i.e. the different colours) to add decoration to the urn. Crepe paper is wonderfully flexible and stretches very easily around the curve of the handle.

4

Using the drill, make a hole in the middle of the wooden block base 7 cm (2¼ in) deep and just large enough to slot the dowel in. Pour some glue directly into this hole and push the dowel firmly in.

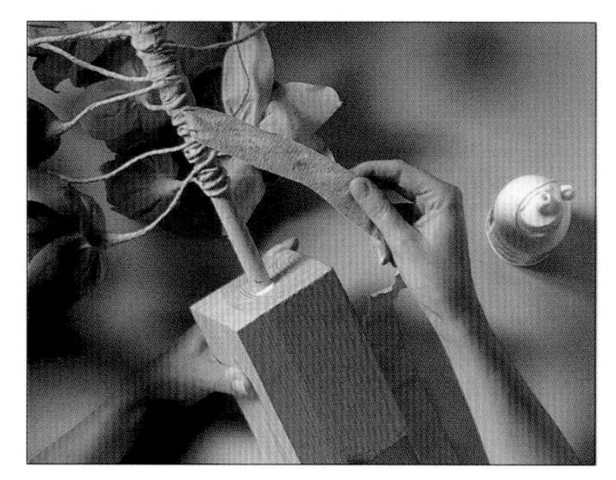

5

Cut the duotone crepe paper into strips 3 cm (1¼ in) wide. Smear some glue onto the dowel 'stem' and, starting from the top, wind the paper around it tightly making sure that the stem is evenly covered right down to the point where the stem reaches the wooden base.

6

Now turn the wand around and carefully arrange all the flowers evenly so that they make a symmetrical shape. This is easy to do as the flower stems are made from copper wire which is firm but very flexible.

10

Put a generous amount of glue onto the front of the wooden block and stick the paper and card urn into place. To help it adhere more firmly, turn it over and place it face-down on a table with the flower section overhanging the edge. Put a heavy weight on the block for about 30 minutes until the glue has set.

Enlarge this template to 200% on a photocopier.

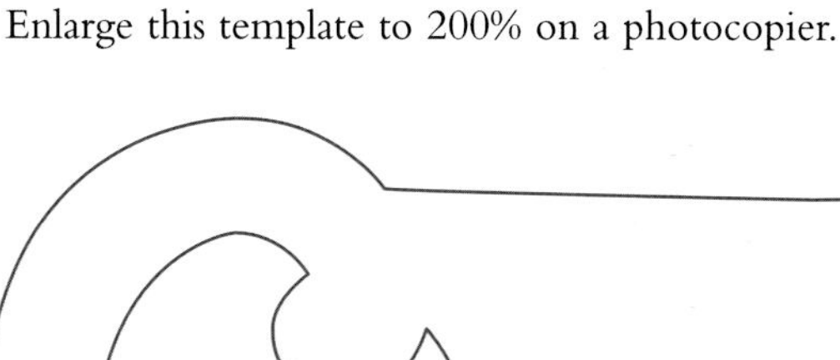

Laundry Box

THIS LAUNDRY BOX has been decorated using the traditional European papercutting techniques of folding and cutting symmetrical images. The urn of flowers is a favourite motif found in different forms in peasant art throughout the world, appearing on painted furniture, carved into wooden implements and embroidered onto intricate costumes.

Peasant artists viewed paper as a rare and valuable commodity and they found many ways to re-use it, often transforming it into striking images used to decorate the home. This age-old impulse of seeking out and preserving scrap paper can bring us rich rewards today.

The papers used in this project are either scraps or sheets of inexpensive recycled paper. The restrained range of colours and simple stylized image are reminiscent of combinations often found in the Swedish country style of decoration.

MATERIALS

- White cartridge paper
- Laundry box
- Paper clips
- Pencil
- Templates (see page 27)
- Recycled paper in shades of brown, yellow and tan
- Small scissors
- Small circular pot lid (to use as a template)
- Pinking shears
- Wallpaper paste (fungicide free)
- Bowl for the paste
- Ruler
- Matt acrylic varnish and brush

1

Fold the white cartridge paper in half and place the template along the fold. Hold it in place with paper clips. Using a sharp pencil, draw around the template carefully, remove the template and cut around the drawn lines.

2

Using the small scissors, carefully cut small 'v' shaped nicks into the circles which are to become the flowers. If you are nervous about cutting them freehand, draw them in first with a pencil.

3

Cut two more white flowers from the same paper and put aside. Use a pot lid or something similar as a template to make nine tan coloured petals. These need to be slightly smaller than the flower shapes on the larger pot of flowers.

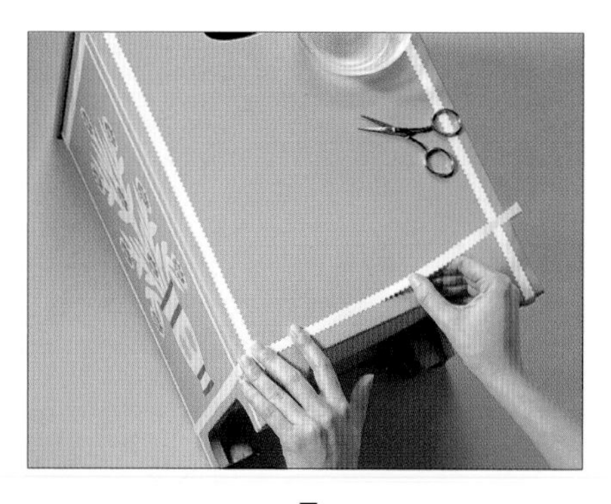

5

Cut strips of white paper approximately 1 cm (½ in) wide with the pinking shears. Smear them evenly with the ready mixed wallpaper paste and position as a border around the box 1 cm (½ in) from each edge.

6

Smear the paste over the pot of flowers motif, taking care at this point not to tear the intricately cut paper as it is delicate when wet. It is a good idea to smear a small amount of paste directly onto the painted box. Lay the motif down carefully in the central position and smooth over with your fingers to expel extra paste and air bubbles.

7

Paste and place the two extra white flowers equidistantly along the central stem. Next, paste the tan coloured petals into the centre of each flower. Finally, cut some small yellow circles and paste centrally onto each flower.

4

Using the ruler and pencil, lightly mark the centre of the box panel. This is in order to place the motif in the correct position and to make the design symmetrical.

8

Cut some strips of the brown paper using the pinking shears and decorate the vase as shown. The top and base strip have one pinked and one straight edge. Cut two yellow petal motifs and paste centrally onto the vase. Leave overnight to allow the paste to dry thoroughly, then varnish with three or four coats of matt acrylic varnish.

Enlarge these templates on a photocopier to suit the size of your laundry box.

Bloomsbury Table

THIS USEFUL LITTLE SIDE TABLE is partly inspired by the work of the Omega workshops. These were a number of English artists connected to the famous Bloomsbury literary group who came together to apply their work and ideas to decorative pieces. The workshops, which started in 1913, were inspired by the French Post-Impressionists and the decorative arts movements in Europe. Their products brought about a radical new taste in England and the Omega legacy was and is carried on in the work of subsequent artists and designers in the field of furniture, textiles, wallpaper and carpet design.

Although it is perfectly possible to decorate an unpainted table, it is much more satisfying to find a pretty, old or ready-made version to decorate. The one used here was bought from a large chain of shops and the top has been painted a dull purple-grey to complement the original yellow of the table, still seen on the legs. The design is extremely simple and only two new colours are introduced – a crisp white for the leaves and a shade of yellow for the stylized leaf veins. Leaves were a favourite Omega motif.

MATERIALS

- Large sheet of white cartridge paper, 100 gsm
- Yellow origami paper or any scrap paper
- Templates (see page 31)
- Pinking shears
- Large compass
- Paper clips
- Small scissors
- Small round table – the one used here has a diameter of 60 cm (24 in)
- Wallpaper paste (fungicide-free)
- Bowl for the paste
- Sponge
- Acrylic varnish
- Brush

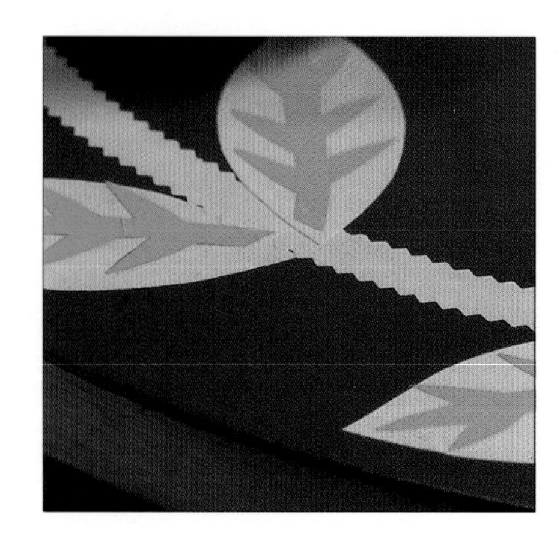

1

Lay the large piece of white paper over the top of the table and mark a circle by pressing the overlapping part over the edge of the table to make a clear fold line. Cut around this line and fold the circle into four as shown.

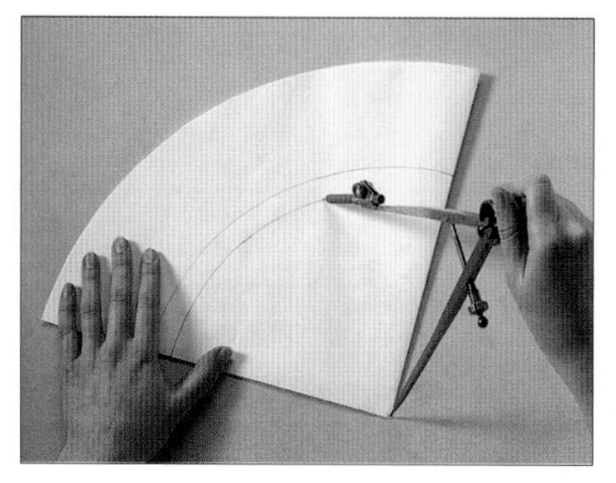

2

Take the compass with a radius of approximately 20 cm (8 in), put the point into the corner of the circle and draw an arc. Then increase the radius and draw another arc 2 cm (¾ in) above the first.

3

Use the pinking shears to cut out this curved strip which, when carefully opened up, forms a large circle.

5

Mix up the wallpaper paste and smear a ring of it around the table top. Open up the pinked circular strip and lay down evenly onto the pasted area. Smooth gently with your fingers to expel any air bubbles or extra paste.

6

Paste the white leaves in 12 pairs either side of the circular strip, making sure they are evenly spaced. Smooth them to expel any air or spare paste.

7

Paste the yellow leaf veins carefully onto the leaves. Wipe away the glue with a damp sponge and, when dry, give three or four coats of acrylic varnish for extra protection.

4

Clip the leaf vein template onto the yellow paper, draw around and cut out 24 leaf veins. Cut out 24 leaves from the white paper in this way.

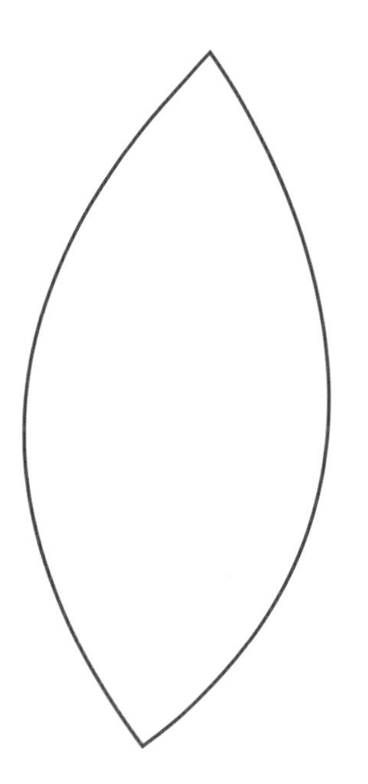

Enlarge these templates on a photocopier to suit the size of your table.

Picture Frame

THIS CHARMING PICTURE FRAME made entirely from paper and card has been inspired by Caribbean architecture where houses and churches are frequently inventively constructed from corrugated iron. This is often painted in the bright colours so prevalent in hot countries. They are usually adorned with fretwork bargeboarding with simple interpretations of 'baroque' decorative features applied to door and window frames.

The base or background of the frame shown here is made from a white corrugated card called microboard, the type with narrow grooves. The three-dimensional surface decoration in a contrasting colour has been created from cut, scored and folded paper. Scoring and bending flat shapes to make three-dimensional forms is the basis of the craft of paper sculpture. In its purest form, white paper or card is always used and it is quite amazing to see what it is possible to make with this particular technique. Once you have successfully made the frame you may be inspired enough to go on to make other decorative objects for the home. The adventurous might attempt a whole cupboard!

MATERIALS

White corrugated microboard

Craft knife

Cutting mat

Metal ruler

Fine pen

Plate

Scrap cardboard

Double-sided tape

White glue

Spatula

Pink coverboard, 300 gsm

Pinking shears

Templates (see page 34)

Paper clips

Scissors

Scoring tool, such as a knitting needle

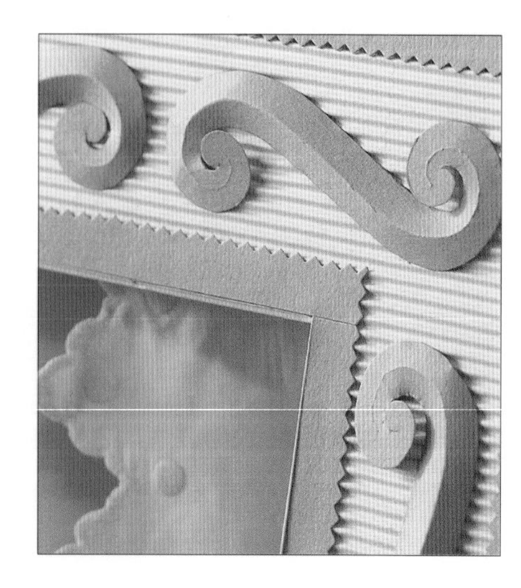

1

Using the craft knife and cutting mat, cut a microboard rectangle measuring 25 x 34 cm (10 x 13½ in). Measure a point 28 cm (11 in) along the longer sides and draw a line across. Draw an arc on the top section using a plate as a template. Draw a border 7.5 cm (3 in) wide around the rectangle and cut away the central section.

2

Cut an identically shaped piece from the scrap cardboard and stick to the microboard using double-sided tape.

3

Cut strips of the microboard just wide enough to cover the raw edges around the inside and outside of the frame. Stick in place with the white glue, taking care not to get the glue on the front of the frame.

7

Turn the pieces over and bend back carefully away from the scored lines to create the three-dimensional effect.

8

Stick the urn centrally onto the top section of the frame with its base resting on the top pinked strip. Stick the leaf shapes either side, attaching them to the frame and the urn with two small dabs of glue.

Enlarge these templates on a photocopier to 218%

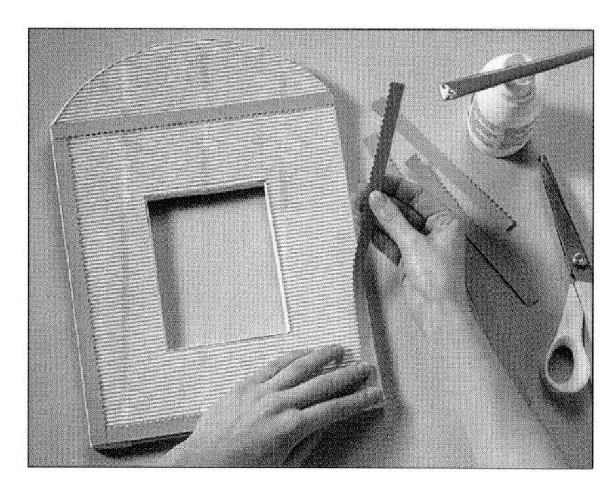

4

Cut strips of the pink coverboard 1.5 cm (¾ in) wide and cut down one side with the pinking shears. Stick around the rectangular part of the frame with the zigzagged edge facing inwards

5

Attach the templates to the pink card with paper clips and draw around them carefully with the fine pen. Cut out with the small scissors.

6

Lay the cut-out pieces on the cutting mat and score the lines as indicated on the templates.

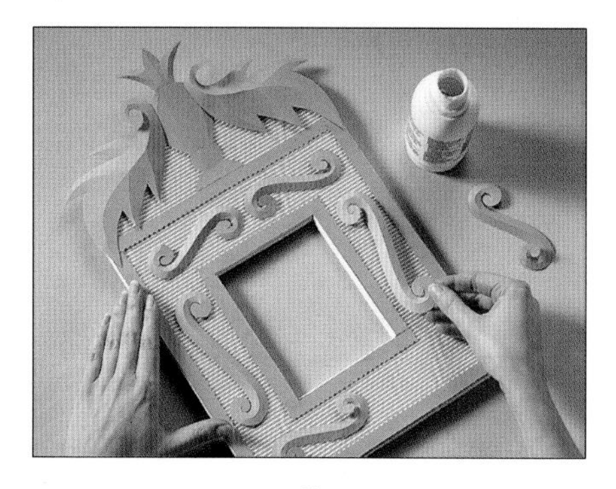

9

Finally, stick the scrolls on in the same way, using two small dabs of glue at either end and two in the middle where the folded sides touch the frame. It is important not to get any glue on the frame itself.

Decorated Tray

THIS TRAY IS DECORATED using the most traditional of papercutting techniques – folding and cutting. This simple technique, employing a fundamental design principle – that of symmetry and balance – is the most commonly used approach in papercutting. It appears predominantly in European folk art, particularly in the rural mountain areas of Switzerland, where it was carried out almost exclusively by the menfolk.

Here, very beautiful and intricate examples of papercuts or *Scherenschnitte* are still produced although the older examples have a quality and charm which is difficult to surpass. They were mainly cut from black paper and mounted on white, although there are interesting examples cut from patterned or gold paper. The imagery always reflected the life of the farmer or peasant, with popular images including houses, mountains, churches, trees and animals.

The other country famous for its tradition of papercutting is Poland where the work became more and more colourful with the introduction of coloured glacé papers in the second half of the nineteenth century.

MATERIALS

- Blank tray with sloping sides
- Recycled white paper
- Scissors
- Pencil
- Pinking shears
- Small circular lid to use as template for scalloped edge
- Hole puncher
- Cellulose wallpaper paste (fungicide free)
- Bowl for paste
- Paper clips
- Card for templates of house, trees and birds (see page 39)
- Cutting mat
- Ruler
- Blue and white patterned paper
- Rubber
- Craft knife
- Matt varnish
- Paintbrush

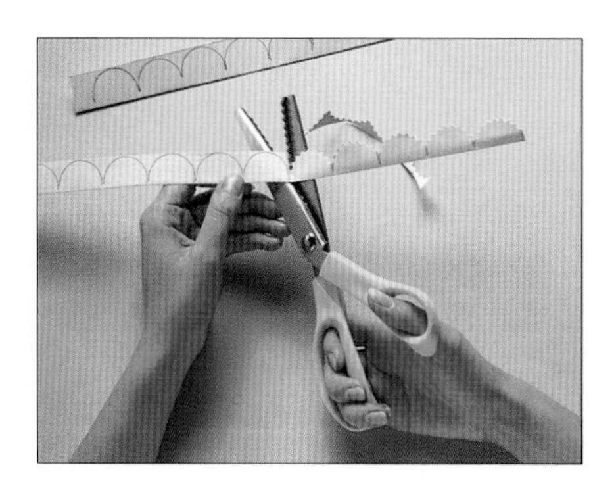

1

Cut a strip of white paper 5 cm (2 in) wide and slightly longer than the tray's longer edge. Cut another strip slightly longer than the shorter edge. Fold these strips in half lengthways and trace around the lid to make a line of semi-circles. Cut around the scalloped edge with pinking shears.

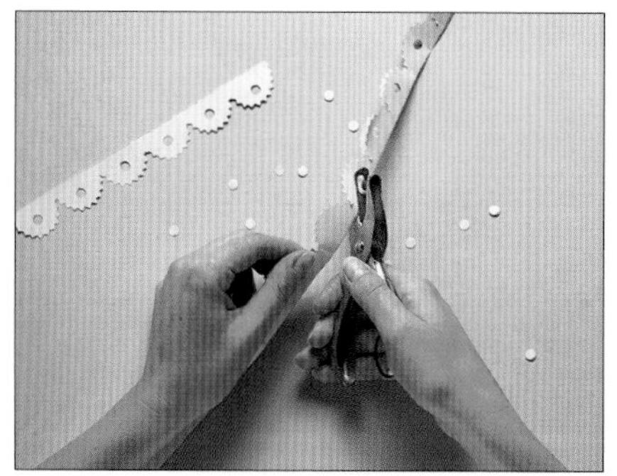

2

Using the hole puncher, make a hole in the centre of each scallop. When you have made all the holes, cut along the folded edge with scissors or a craft knife. These strips form the outer decorative edging.

3

Mix the wallpaper paste according to the packet's instructions and put a small amount into a bowl. Trim the decorative strips to fit exactly along the edges of the tray base. Using your fingers, smear the paste lightly along the edges of the tray base and also onto the underside of the paper. Lay the paper in place, pressing firmly with your fingers to eliminate any air bubbles.

5

Smear the tray where the house will be placed with paste. Unfold the house and smear the back lightly with paste. Place in the centre of the tray and smooth out any air bubbles. The paper may bubble as the wet paste stretches it, but it will dry smooth.

6

Paste the trees in place in the same way. When sticking the branches ensure they lie flat on the tray without tearing. Using the patterned paper, cut two wing shapes for the birds, making sure you have a variety of tones in the pieces. Stick into position on each bird.

7

Using pinking shears, cut long strips 1 cm (½ in) wide from the patterned paper to decorate the front of the house. First, stick the vertical pieces between the windows; next, the horizontal strips at the bottom and middle; finally, add the two side pieces. Cut a scalloped and punched strip (to match the border around the edge) and stick in place to form the eaves. Save some punched holes to use for door handles and for the birds' eyes.

4

Cut out a house template. Fold a piece of white paper in half, place the 'middle' of the house against the fold and secure with paper clips. On the cutting mat cut around the template with the craft knife. Cut out the trees and birds in the same way. Using the pencil and ruler, mark the centre of the tray so the house can be positioned centrally.

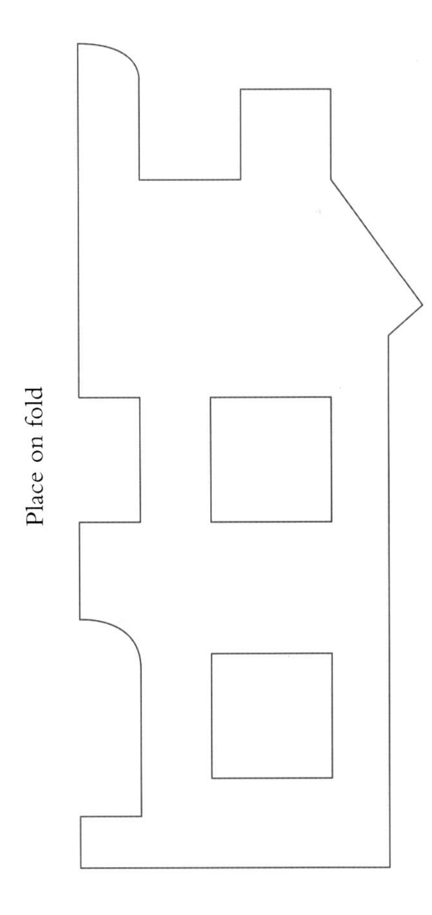

Enlarge these templates on a photocopier to suit the size of your tray.

8

Cut thinner strips of white paper with pinking shears and stick in place to form the window cross-bars and double door. Cut narrow strips from the patterned paper with the pinking shears for the star on the dome. Cut small squares to stick on the chimneys. Decorate the pots with bands of pinked paper and stick a tapering strip along the tree trunk. When the glue has dried, rub out the pencil marks and apply two coats of varnish.

Snowflake Sewing Box

ALMOST EVERYONE'S EXPERIENCE of papercutting goes back to childhood and making simple snowflakes cut with scissors from a circle of white paper at Christmas-time. These were often displayed in classroom windows and they remain to this day some of the most beautiful and satisfying objects to make from cut paper.

The real magic lies in the fact that the circle is folded into eight and the design is cut away from this small section. When the snowflake is unfolded, the evenness of the design and its symmetry are always a surprise. The sense of order and achievement gained from this kind of activity is also deeply satisfying. The circular form fits beautifully onto the lid of this round wooden box and the side is decorated by making a simple trellis-work band in the same paper. The design works best when the clean white paper is pasted onto a contrasting darker colour.

MATERIALS

Painted wooden box, diameter 20 cm (8 in), depth 10 cm (4 in)

White cartridge paper, 118 gsm

Scissors

Template (see page 43)

Paper clips

Fine pen

Craft knife

Cutting mat

Metal ruler

Wallpaper paste (fungicide free)

Bowl for the paste

Acrylic varnish

Brush

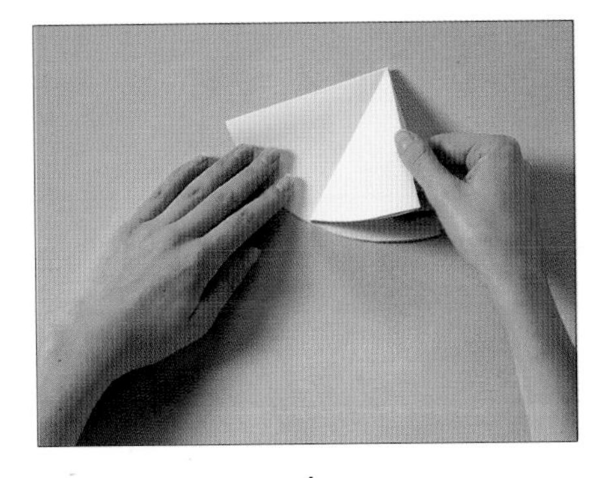

1

Cut out a circle of the cartridge paper 20 cm (8 in) in diameter or the same size as the lid of the box (it is easiest to place the lid on the paper and draw around it). Fold the paper four times to make eight sections by folding in half, then into quarters and then fold each quarter back on itself to make the division into eighths. This method of folding ensures more accurate cutting.

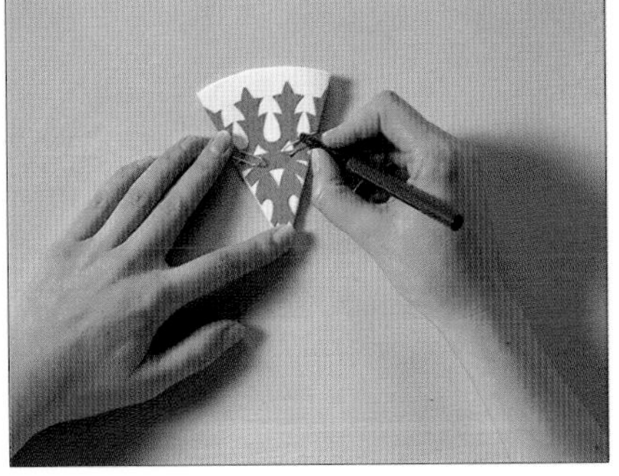

2

Lay the template on the folded circle and hold in place with paper clips. Draw carefully around the shape with the pen to transfer the design ready for cutting.

3

Lay the marked and folded paper on the cutting mat and use the craft knife to cut away the areas indicated. You will need to press firmly for the knife to cut through all the layers. If you find this too difficult to do all at once, cut a few layers at a time. Even if the knife does not cut all the way through you will find that it marks the layers beneath to serve as a new template.

5

Place the strip on the cutting mat and cut away these triangles on either side using the craft knife. At this stage you need to be careful and accurate, so take your time.

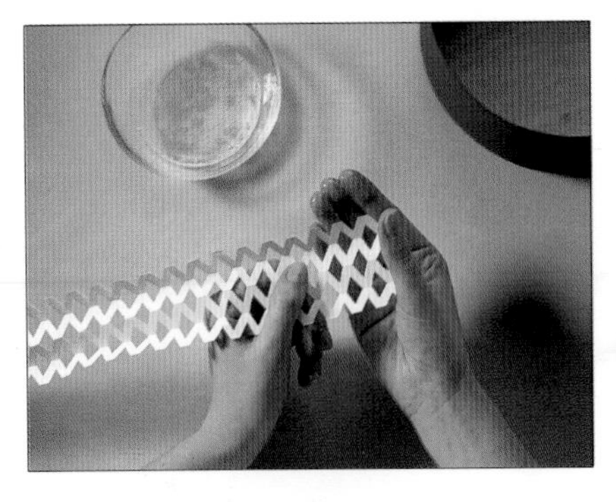

6

When you have finished cutting, open out the strip to reveal the even trellis pattern. Mix up the wallpaper paste according to the instructions and smear a thin layer on both sides of the paper. Stick in place around the side of the box and smooth with your fingers to expel any surplus glue or air bubbles. Trim to match at the join.

7

Open out the snowflake and smear with paste on both sides, as with the trellis strip. Place carefully on the centre of the lid and smooth with your fingers to release any excess paste or air bubbles. Allow the paste to dry overnight, then paint with two coats of protective acrylic varnish.

4

Cut a strip of the paper long enough to go round the side of the box and 6 cm (2½ in) deep. Fold into four lengthways, concertina-style, and mark a series of parallel lines along it at regular angles with the pen and the metal ruler. Complete by marking identical lines angled in the other direction. These should meet at the edges, leaving triangles of exactly the same size in-between.

Enlarge this template on a photocopier to 123%

Lighting

Paper is endlessly adaptable and now that it is available in so many different forms, it is possible to achieve varied and wonderful effects. The following projects give you the opportunity to try some of the well-known traditional techniques, such as cutting, folding, piercing and punching, which have been used to create stunning, contemporary lights and lanterns.

Star Light

TRADITIONALLY, LAMPSHADES have always been made from paper and it is not difficult to see why. It is such a versatile material and can be easily cut, folded, rolled, punched or pierced. It can be used on a small scale or can be assembled into much larger pieces. With the growing variety of types of paper available from a wide number of sources, the design possibilities increase tremendously and the translucent or opaque qualities of paper can be exploited, as well as its innate strength.

These striking lanterns are based on a simple geometric form. Holes have been punched through the paper to create a design which is emphasized by the restrained use of plain paper. This gives the lights a serene quality, but it would be interesting to experiment and construct the lanterns from coloured or patterned paper, which would allow the star to glow when the light was switched on.

MATERIALS

Template (see page 127)

2 sheets of card, 250 gsm, in natural colour

Sharp pencil

Scissors

Scoring tool

Ruler

Double-sided tape or paper glue

Hole punchers with two different sizes of holes

Small stapler

Electric cable and low-watt bulb

Pipe cleaner

1

Lay the template on page 127 onto the card and draw around with the sharp pencil. Make a little mark where all the fold lines meet. Cut out with scissors. You will need five sections cut this way.

2

Use the scoring tool or improvise with a dry ballpoint pen to score along the lines which are shown on the template in order to accentuate the internal fold lines and those delineating the fold-in tabs.

3

Fold along and away from these scored lines in order to make one section of the star. Fold the tabs inwards as shown.

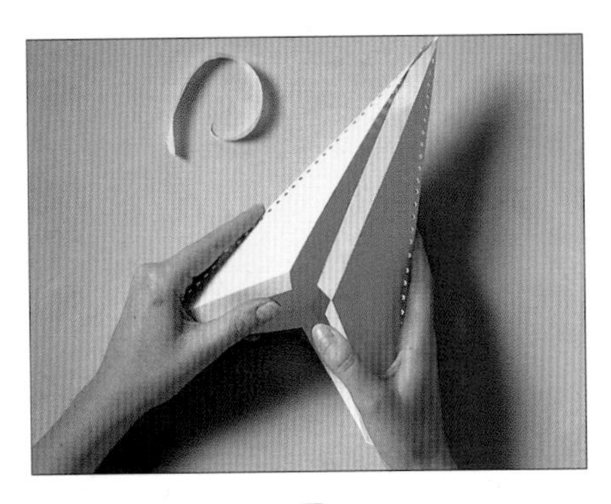

5

Fold back into the starpoint shape and stick a length of double-sided tape onto the folded over tab. Push this under the opposite side and stick both sides together firmly. At this point you can put your hand into the point and press the join from outside.

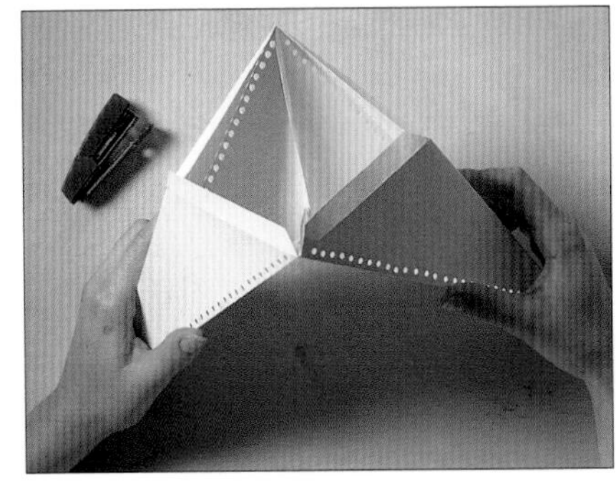

6

Make four more points in this manner so that you have five in all. Place two together so that the punched and unpunched sides match up and staple the matching tabs three times along each side. You can also glue or tape to make the join stronger. Secure all five points together in this way, leaving the last join open.

7

Make two holes with the larger hole punch exactly opposite each other either side of the opening. This is where the electric cable and bulb will be inserted.

4

Fold and hold the long sides together and, using the smaller of the two hole punchers, punch an even line of holes.

8

Thread the cable and bulb (which must be a small 40 watt one) through the slit. Thread the pipe cleaner through these two holes and twist together to hold the star in the correct position.

Oak Leaf Light

IT IS ALWAYS SATISFYING TO WORK with designs from the natural world and this is a predominant theme in folk or peasant art. The enduring and easily recognisable shape of the oak leaf has been used here to create a really contemporary effect.

This striking light shade has been simply made by employing three traditional techniques of working with paper - those of folding, cutting and punching. The shade itself is free-standing and the light source could be a low watt bulb fitted into a free-standing holder or a number of candles protected by placing them in glass jars. As the paper used is so thick, the effect created is a combination of the subtle light escaping from the cut slits and punched holes and the more dynamic light cast backwards against the wall behind. For the best effect it should be used in an uncluttered environment.

MATERIALS

Sheet cotton rag paper 640 gsm in yellow ochre

Metal ruler

Craft knife

Cutting mat

Template (see below)

Sharp H pencil

Bradawl

Small plank of wood

1

Cut a piece of the yellow paper measuring 26 x 36 cm (10½ x 15 in), then use the pencil and the ruler to mark top and bottom into six strips each 6 cm (2½ in) wide.

2

Place the ruler on the card at the points marked. Cut gently and very slightly into the thickness of the card with the craft knife to make the folding easier. With very thick card it may be necessary to repeat this shallow cut on the back as well, following the identical line. Cut five lines in total.

4

Lay the template onto the three backward turning folds and draw around it neatly using the sharp pencil.

5

Lay the card onto the cutting mat and cut through the right-hand side of the leaf shape only, finishing the cut neatly at the fold.

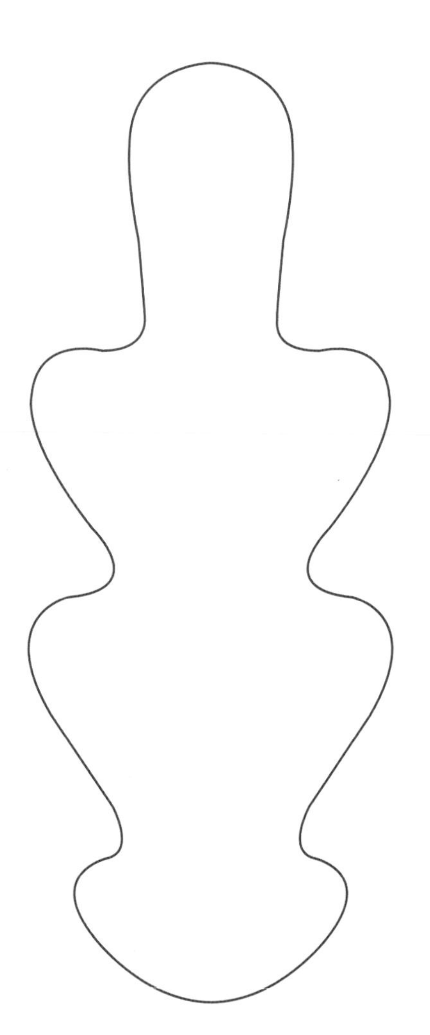

Enlarge this template on a photocopier to 168%

3

Fold the card away from the two outside lines and the middle line. This may be difficult as the card is so thick but try to fold as evenly as possible. Gently fold the two remaining score lines inwards.

6

Place the card onto the block of wood and with the bradawl pierce even holes along the uncut side of the leaf shape.

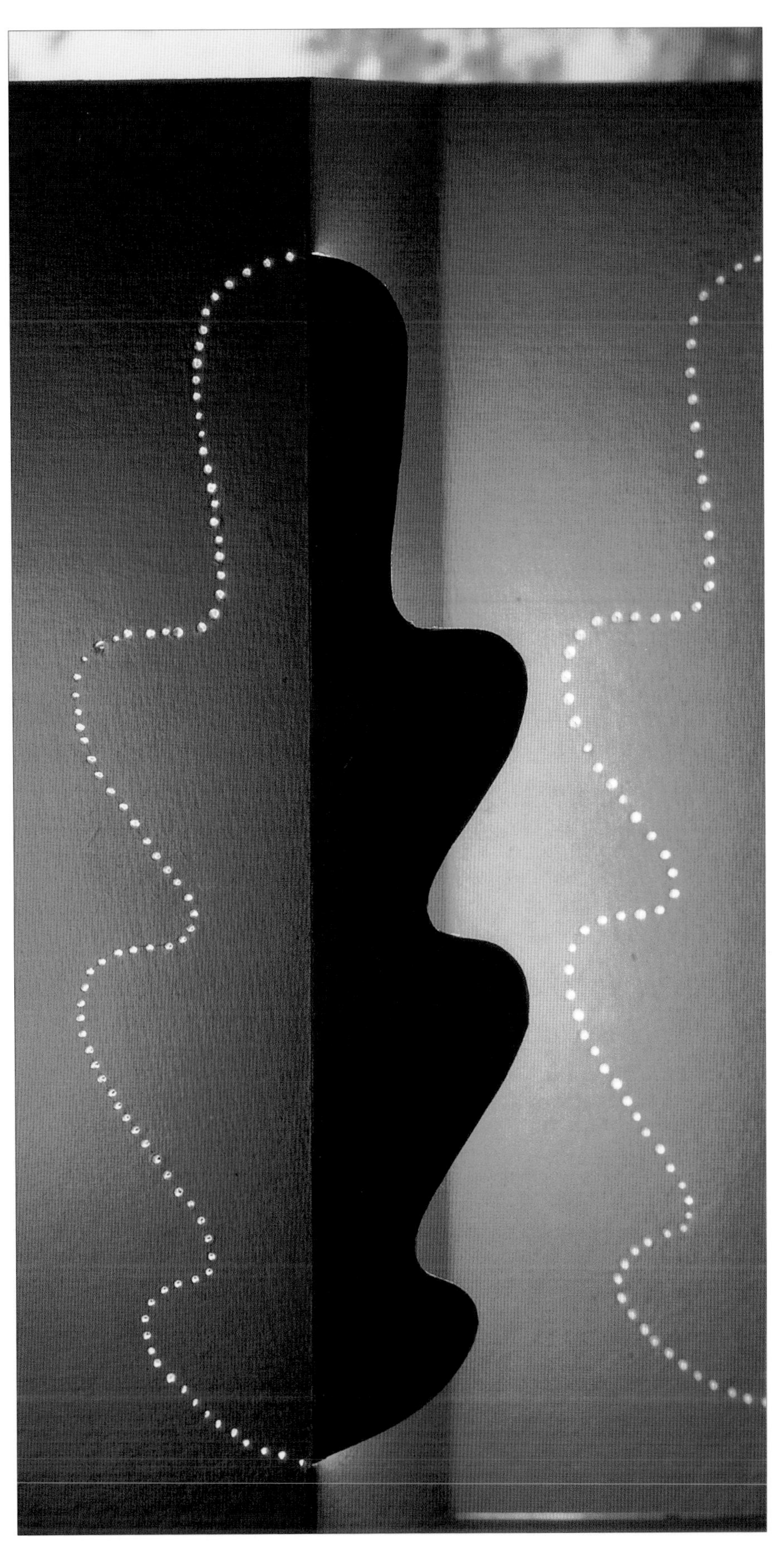

Pinpricked Lampshade

Here the papercut and the lampshade itself are tonally the same shade and colour and it is only when the light is switched on that the full effect of this lovely project is seen. The circular design has been cut from a round piece of paper folded into eight, snowflake-style, and the delicate pinpricked decoration is easy to do as long as you have some patience - it is best not to hurry when doing this project.

The motifs of hearts, birds and leaves are commonly found in peasant art and the effective technique of enhancing the design by pinpricking an even pattern all around the edge is commonly found in American folk art, in Shaker crafts. Although this technique is ideally suited to use on a lampshade, it could be equally well displayed against a window or serve as an unusual picture in a frame, especially if an inscription was added.

MATERIALS

- Strathmore grandee ivory paper, 90 gsm
- Plate as template 23 cm (9 in) in diameter
- Fine pen
- Scissors
- Craft knife
- Cutting mat
- Paper clips
- Sharp pointed bradawl
- Plank of wood
- White glue
- Lampshade

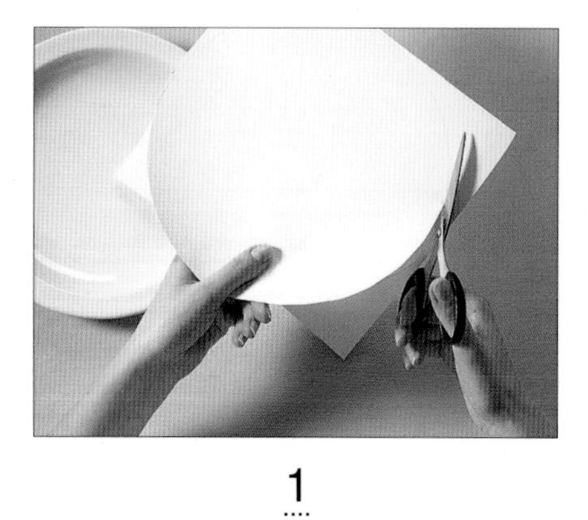

1

Place the plate upside down onto a piece of the paper and use as a template to draw around, making a circle 23 cm (9 in) in diameter.

2

Fold the paper in half, then into quarters and finally fold each free quarter back on itself to create eighths. As with the sewing box on page 42, never fold more than two layers at once as this makes for greater accuracy in cutting.

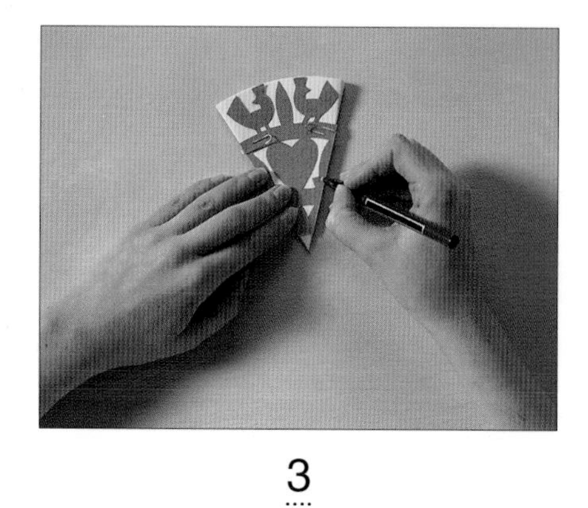

3

Lay the template on the folded paper and hold in place with the paper clips. Draw around the design accurately in pen.

Enlarge this template on a photocopier to 127%

4

Remove the template and place the marked and folded paper on the cutting mat. Cut away the marked areas as shown, paying particular attention to the internal sections.

5

Unfold the design and place the circular papercut onto a block of soft wood. Using the tip of the bradawl, punch small holes all around the design, down the centre of the hearts and leaves and around the edges of the circular strips. Carefully smear the back of the papercut with glue and stick onto a lampshade.

Pierced and Punched Lanterns

MANY PEOPLE WILL REMEMBER making similar lanterns from their early schooldays, and this remains a particularly suitable project to make with children. Nothing could be easier or simpler to create than these pretty lanterns. They are made from a pad of subtle coloured recycled paper – these are readily available from good stationery shops and are quite inexpensive. Each sheet is folded three times and the pattern created by using a hole puncher, scissors or pinking shears while the paper is folded.

When the finished lantern is carefully placed over a nightlight (placed inside a jam jar for safety's sake), the warm glow of the subtle colours and the patterns of light cast through the slits and holes are really quite beautiful.

As these lanterns are so easily made, a collection of them could be assembled to decorate a garden by placing them amongst plants on a still summer night.

MATERIALS

- Sheet of A4 recycled coloured paper
- Hole punch
- Tracing wheel
- Wad of tissue paper
- Ruler
- Pinking shears
- Double-sided tape
- Small scissors
- Jam jar
- Nightlight

1

Fold the paper into fourths lengthwise, This means three fold lines making a zig-zag shape. Use the hole puncher to make a line of holes along the side of the folded paper which has the two cut edges. When you open it up, this makes a single line of neat holes at each edge and a double line along the middle fold.

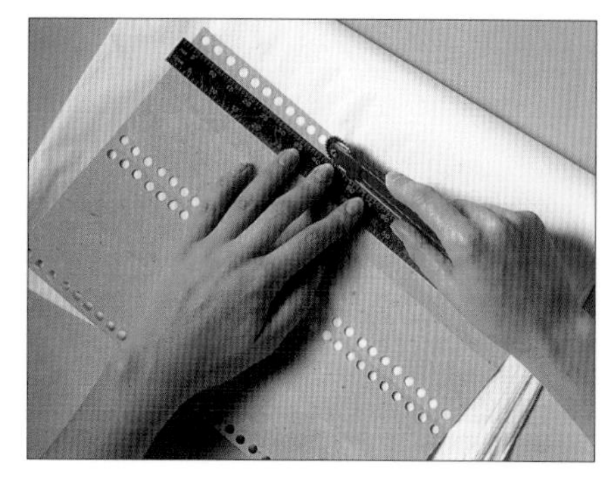

2

Using the wad of tissue paper as a yielding base, place the punched paper over this and make raised dotted lines by wheeling the tracing wheel along the side of the ruler. These lines should be made beside each line of punched holes.

3

Fold the paper again along the original folds, then use the pinking shears to cut a series of cuts at a slant along the folded edge. These need to stop the same distance away from the dotted line as that line is from the punched holes, and 2 cm (¾ in) from each edge.

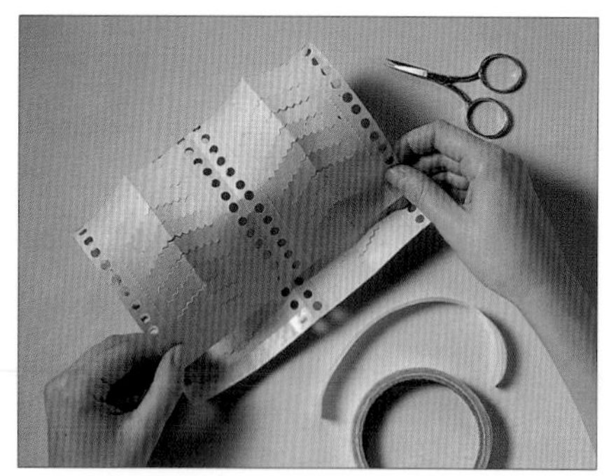

4

Cut a length of double-sided tape and stick it along the inside edge of one end of the lantern. Roll the cylinder over and carefully stick the ends together. When using double sided tape you need to be sure that the paper is positioned carefully before sticking. If you are worried, use paper glue which allows the paper to be repositioned.

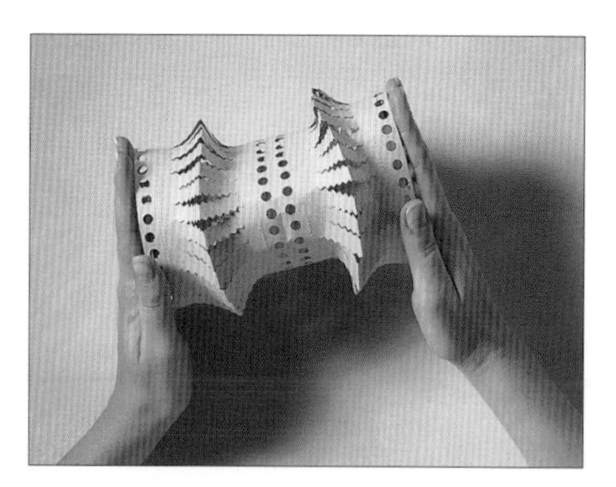

5

Using both hands, gently press the two ends towards each other to accentuate the pinked folds. Sit the nightlight in a jam jar and place inside the lantern.

Dahlia Candle Shades

THE MOST SATISFYING PROJECTS are always those in which the material and technique combine to enhance the design. These refined lampshades are a perfect example of this and, with their stylized flower motif, they have a really professional look to them.

They are easily made with a template, although some care needs to be taken when cutting around the petals. The cut area of the flower is then gently rolled back with the fingers to become three-dimensional and the centre is pushed through to create stamens. The paper is rolled into a cylinder, either with the flowers facing inwards or outwards.

A jam jar containing a nightlight is placed inside and the gently flickering light helps to define the shape and depth of each individual flower. For extra safety, the paper lampshade can be treated with a fire retarding spray. If using an electric light bulb, select one with a low wattage.

MATERIALS

Sheet of thin card, such as Elephant Hide 190 gsm in Ivory
Cutting mat
Sharp pencil
Ruler
Template (see page 67)
Craft knife
Rubber
Paper glue
Paper clips
Jam jar
Nightlight

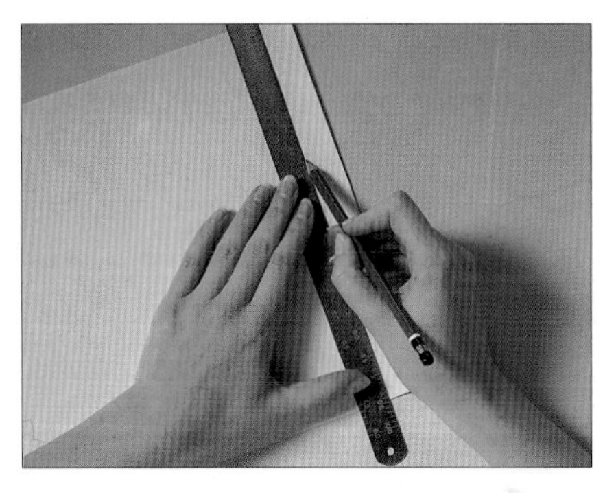

1

Lay the card on the cutting mat and cut a rectangle measuring 25 x 37.5 cm (10 x 14½ in). Using the pencil and ruler, mark off a 2 cm (¾ in) strip along each short edge.

2

Lay the template on the card and mark round in pencil. Space the flowers evenly between the pencil lines at each end, with four rows of three flowers at the outer edges and three rows of two in between.

4

Next, cut a 16-point star in the centre of each flower. Do this by making eight cuts. If you are nervous about cutting this part of the design freehand, then mark it first with the pencil.

5

Rub out all the pencil marks very carefully. Then, using your finger and thumb, pull up each separate petal and curl slightly so that they are raised towards you. Push gently with your finger through the star in the centre of the flower to create the stamens.

3

Using the craft knife, cut around the petals, leaving a small uncut section where each petal meets in the centre. This is essential because cutting all around would mean that the whole flower falls out.

6

Roll the paper loosely into a cylinder shape with the flowers projecting outwards. Put some paper glue along the marked strip to stick the two ends together. Secure with the two paper clips until the glue is set. Sit the nightlight in the jam jar and place inside the shade.

A different effect can be obtained by rolling the card into a cylinder with the flowers facing inwards. This makes a more subtle shaded effect when the light shines through.

Use the template at this size.

Celebrations

Brightly coloured paper decorations are often a feature at festive occasions in many different cultures. Many of these decorations are quick to create and these projects demonstrate that paper works equally well when used in two or three dimensions. The flat sheet is simply transformed by folding and cutting or weaving to produce stunning flowers, garlands, pictures or baskets.

Valentine Picture

THIS LOVER'S GREETING or memento of a special friendship has been created in the enduring form of a papercut picture. The heart motif is a potent and favourite one in the folk art of many cultures, but especially in Scandinavia and central Europe. The early American settlers from these regions took their skills and cultural references with them, and so the heart has become one of the dominant images in American folk art.

The heart design in this project, however, has been more inspired by Switzerland. Here papercutting is an intricate and detailed artform, often using folded black paper. The symmetrical form of the heart was often used as it lent itself so beautifully to traditional folding techniques. Another universal and enduring symbol used is that of the tree of life, a powerful and optimistic image. Here, the two birds provide a more peaceful theme.

This picture has been made from scraps of different papers. It is well worth building up a collection of old wrapping paper, stamps, letters, glittery sweet wrappers and hand-painted paper – the possibilities for using them are endless.

THE YOUNG LADIES' JOURNAL.

MATERIALS

Yellow handmade Indian paper

Poster paper in purple and mauve

Patterned paper in blue, red, orange and purple

Patterned gold paper (Chinese New Year money)

Ruler

Pencil

Small scissors

Templates (see page 126)

Paper glue

Paper clips

Cutting mat

Craft knife

Rubber

1

Using a craft knife and cutting mat, cut the yellow background paper into a rectangle 25 x 35 cm (10 x 14 in). With the pencil and ruler, lightly mark a 2 cm (¾ in) border all around the edge. Cut two blocks 5.5 x 6.5 cm (2¼ x 2¾ in) from purple paper and two from mauve paper and stick them at the base corners. Cut a strip of red patterned paper 2.5 cm (1 in) wide and stick this between these blocks.

2

Fold two small pieces of the gold patterned paper in half together and place the straight edge of the heart template against the fold of the paper. Hold in place using a paper clip. Cut out two hearts with the small scissors and stick in place onto the corner blocks.

6

Mark the centre of the paper using a ruler and pencil. Open out the heart, carefully glue up the back and place in position on the picture using the central vertical pencil line as a guide. The base of the heart needs to be 3.5 cm (1¾ in) from the base strip of patterned paper.

7

Fold a piece of the orange patterned paper and use the bird template to cut out two birds. They must be cut together from a folded piece of paper as they need to be mirror images of each other. Stick in place either side of the heart standing on the base strip. Add gold wings and purple eyes to finish.

8

Finally, cut a crown from the purple patterned paper using the template provided on page 126. Stick above the central heart motif and add the elongated gold oval. Very gently rub out all the pencil lines, taking particular care not to touch or damage any of the papercut images.

3

Cut out two pots freehand from the same patterned paper that was used for the base strip and stick in place on top of the corner blocks.

4

Fold a piece of the blue patterned paper in half and hold the template in place with the paper clips. Draw around carefully with a sharp pencil, remove the template and cut out the design with the scissors. Make two such trees, open out and stick in place above the pots.

5

Fold a piece of purple poster paper in half and place the central heart template against the fold. Hold in place with paper clips. Draw round with a pencil and cut out with scissors. Place on the cutting mat and cut out the intricate inner pattern with a craft knife.

Easter Eggs

THE SMOOTH SHELLED FORM of the egg is one of the most beautiful shapes to be found in the natural world. Its deeply satisfying symmetrical form, in effect an elongated sphere, lends itself to a variety of decorative effects. Because of this and its everyday availability, egg decoration features in folk cultures around the world. One of the most famous of these occurs in Poland where eggs are decorated by women with wax, painted or engraved. Some simply coloured eggs are even threaded into the elaborate spider Girandoles (see page 10).

The shape of the egg itself imposes to some extent the style of design and the longitudinal division into quarters, such as is shown in the project here, is very commonly used. The universal motif of a branch or developing leaves, a symbol of new life is particularly common in Polish peasant culture. Goose eggs have been used here because the white shell is very strong, making them good for blowing, and their large, often elongated shape provides a larger surface to decorate. You will find them in farm shops or some country butchers.

MATERIALS

- Blown goose eggs
- Lightweight recycled paper in muted colours such as pink, brown, yellow, orange and blue
- Small scissors
- Paper edgers
- Templates (see page 77)
- Paper clips
- Fine pen
- Wallpaper paste (fungicide-free)
- Bowl for the paste
- Hole puncher
- Clear matt acrylic varnish
- Brush

1

Cut two strips of pink paper approximately 4 mm (1/8 in) wide and long enough to go round the egg lengthways with a little to spare. Also cut four lengths of the brown paper approximately 6 mm (1/4 in) wide after they have been cut down one side with the paper edgers to make a decorative edge.

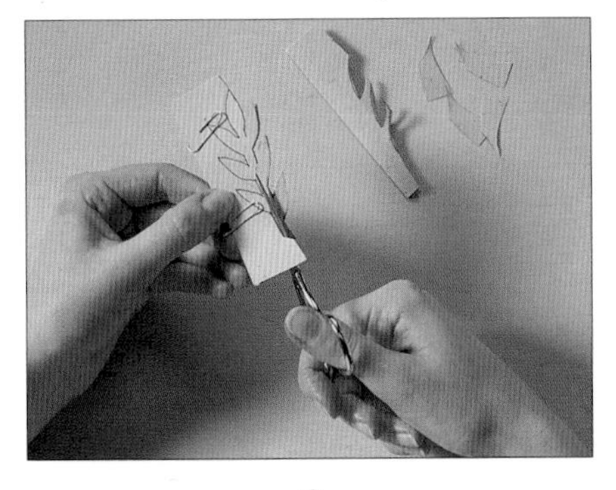

2

Fold the yellow paper into four thicknesses. Clip the template onto the paper. Draw around with the pen, remove the template and cut out four pieces together using the small scissors. You may need to adjust the size of the template to fit your particular egg shape and size.

3

Mix up the wallpaper paste and paste the pink strips around the egg lengthways so that it is divided into four quarters. Now stick the decorative brown strips along side the pink so the straight edges of both colours are parallel.

4

Smear some glue on both sides of the leaf with your fingers and place centrally into the quartered section of the egg. Smooth into place to expel any air bubbles.

5

Cut two eight-petalled flower shapes from the same yellow paper and stick in place over each end of the egg. Punch out two small circles from the brown paper and stick centrally onto the flower shapes. Allow the paste to dry thoroughly, then give the egg two coats of acrylic varnish for extra protection.

Use the template at this size.

Easter Birds

These charming little Easter birds have been cleverly made in three dimensions by sticking two identical pieces of card together along the body, leaving the wings, tail and crown free. Simple techniques such as rolling, cutting, folding and feathering have been used to create this effect. The birds work best when cut from white or ivory paper, and as the shape is so simple, there is no need to complicate the design with the addition of colour.

This kind of design works particularly well as a shadow puppet, especially as the light shines through the punched out eye and the body feathers. To create this magical effect, mount the bird on a slim stick and hold it between a strong light source and a plain background. Other images of people and animals can be cut out and made in a similar way, and a story acted out much in the same way as people did before the advent of passive entertainment. This type of story-telling still takes place in India today.

Although the birds have been used here to adorn an Easter nest, they would make a lovely mobile to suspend over a baby's crib. Alternatively, arrange them around a dense green Christmas tree, each bird carrying a silver-sequinned star in its mouth for a shimmering effect.

MATERIALS

- Cover board, 300 gsm, in china white
- Template (see page 81)
- Pencil
- Small scissors
- Paper glue
- Knitting needle
- Craft knife
- Cutting mat
- Hole puncher

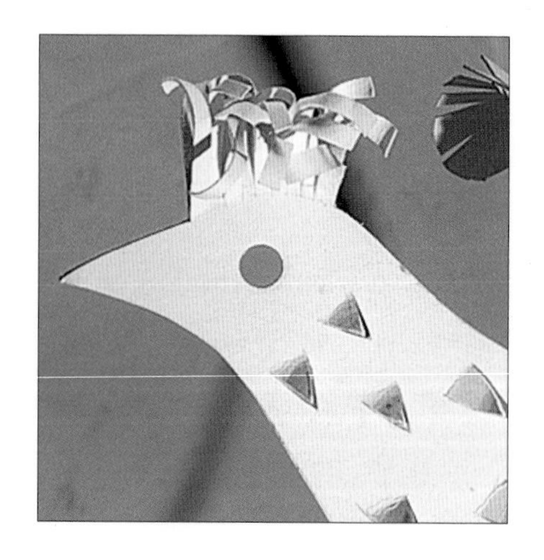

1

Lay the bird template on the paper, draw around with the pencil and cut out neatly with the small scissors. Cut out a second bird in the same way.

2

Paste the paper glue onto the body of one of the birds, avoiding the wings, crown and tail. Stick the two sides of the bird together and press to ensure they are firmly joined.

3

Using small scissors, cut the crown and tail through the two thicknesses into thin strips. Remember that this area of the bird has not been stuck together with the glue.

5

Using the scissors, make little cuts all around the wing feathers, cutting into the card at a slight angle.

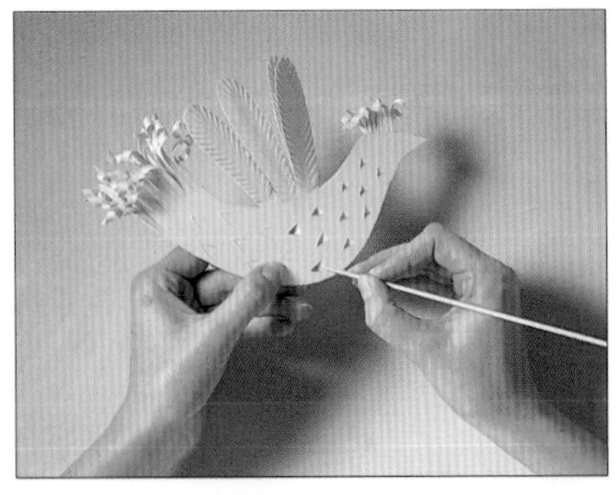

7

Lift the bird up and use the knitting needle to push the cut out sections through to the front of the bird.

4

Roll each individual strip on the tail and crown tightly around the knitting needle to produce a curl. Arrange these curls evenly on each side of the bird.

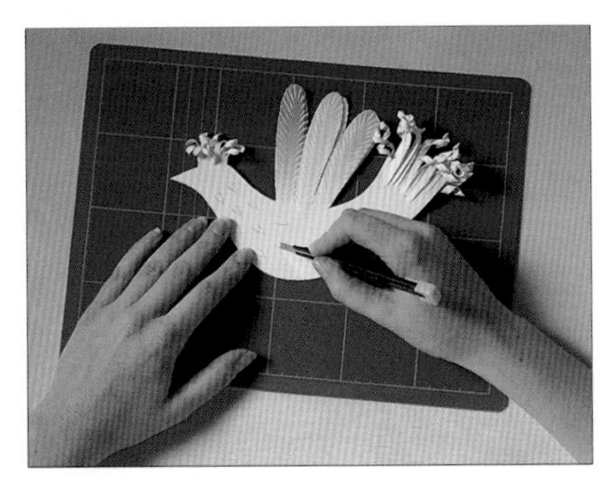

6

Lay the bird on the mat and, with the craft knife, make 'v' shaped cuts along the body, pointing to the tail.

8

Punch a hole as the eye. Arrange the wing feathers into a flying position with three facing each way.

Trace over this outline to make a template.
Cut two birds.

Mexican Ceiling Banners

BEAUTIFUL COLOURED TISSUE BANNERS made in Mexico are used to adorn homes, churches and even graveyards for significant festivals and celebrations. As with many crafts in Mexico, one region, village or sometimes even just one family becomes famous for its skill in a particular craft. San Salvador Huixcolotla, Puebla, is just one such village where banner cutting is a traditional craft passed from generation to generation.

As the craft has developed, the designs have become more intricate. In earlier times the imagery largely consisted of flowers, doves and sacred subjects such as angels or crosses, but over the last few decades the demand has been for ever more entertaining images of skeletons which are used to celebrate the Day of the Dead in early November. Although the banners in the project pictured here are cut with a craft knife, the authentic Mexican banners are punched 50 at a time over a sheet of lead with specially shaped chisels called *fierrtos*. This is an easier method of cutting and certainly more desirable if you need to cut many.

MATERIALS

- Assortment of brightly coloured tissue paper
- Template (see page 87)
- Transparent tape
- Fine pen
- Craft knife
- Cutting mat
- Pinking shears
- Paper clips
- Hole puncher
- Scrap of thin card
- String or thread
- Wallpaper paste (fungicide-free)
- Bowl for the paste

1

Cut three folded sheets of different coloured tissue paper slightly larger than the size of the template. Stick these six layers together along one side with the transparent tape and lay the template on top, holding it in place with paper clips. Draw around the outside and inside all the internal areas with the pen.

2

Remove the template, place the tissue paper on the cutting mat and cut away all the internal areas with the craft knife. Tissue paper is fragile so you need to take care when cutting. It helps to turn the paper rather than the knife to access different angles. Do not cut the small holes in the scalloped edge or in the flower centres.

3

When all the internal areas have been carefully cut away, cut around the scalloped base and the two sides with the pinking shears to make a decorative edge.

4

Because the tissue paper is fragile you need to place a scrap of thin card under the place where the small holes are made with the hole puncher. These are in the middle of each small flower and in the centre of each scalloped edge.

5

Separate the layers and lay one over a piece of scrap paper. Mix the wallpaper paste and smear a little along the top edge of the decoration. The paste should cover the top 1 cm (½ in).

6

Lay the thread along the top edge of the tissue and carefully fold the pasted section over the thread. Run your finger over the double layer so that it adheres firmly to itself. Add more decorations along the same thread, leaving approximately 3 cm (1¼ in) between each piece.

Enlarge this template on a photocopier
to 133%

People Garlands

THE TECHNIQUE OF CUTTING a pattern from evenly folded paper is remembered by most people from their childhood days when it was a favourite infant school activity. Simple garlands of playing children, animals and flowers, often brightly painted, still adorn classroom walls today. This is a most rewarding way of creating decorations – a sort of mass production by hand.

In Mexico, an extraordinarily creative country, many artists seem to play with the intensity of a child, combining their skills with experience to create inventive and extravagant decorations from cut paper. Brightly coloured tissue paper is used, resulting in strings of intricately cut designs used to adorn home and streets alike on festive occasions (see also the project on page 82).

This project has a more North European feel, with eighteenth-century country figures cut from crisp white paper suggesting a wintry or Christmas mood. Try making a row of reindeer or a forest of fir trees and use them to decorate a mantelpiece, a kitchen shelf edge or sit them along the bottom of a window, to be viewed from the outside.

The paper used here needs to be thin enough to cut easily, yet sufficiently strong to enable the garland to stand without support.

MATERIALS

White cartridge paper, 100 gsm

Ruler

Scissors

Templates (see page 91)

Pencil

Paper clips

Craft knife

Cutting mat

Hole punchers, with two different sizes of holes

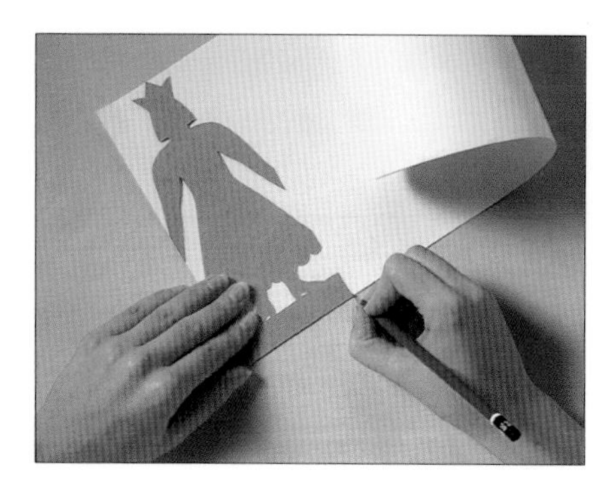

1

Cut a piece of cartridge paper 20 x 85 cm (8 x 33½ in). The easiest way to do this is to cut off the long side of a large sheet of paper. Lay the template on one end of the strip and mark the width of the template base on the paper with a pencil.

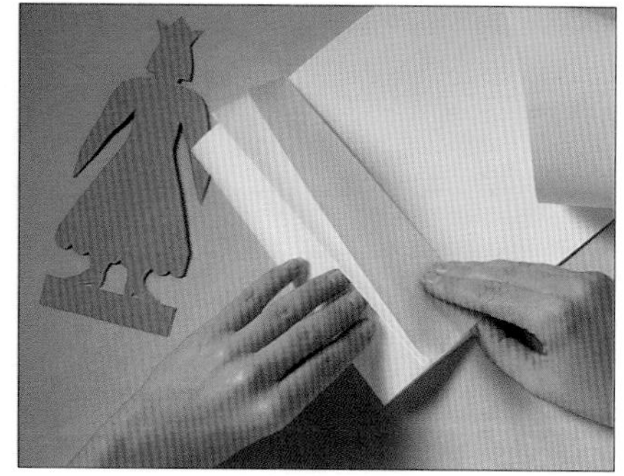

2

Now pleat the paper concertina-style into ten sections, using the pencil mark as your guide. It is important that the paper is folded very evenly.

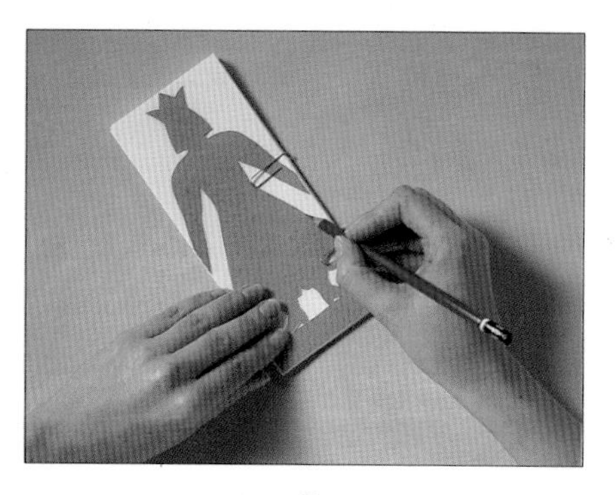

3

Lay the template onto the folded paper and secure with the paper clips. Draw around the shape neatly with the sharp pencil, moving the paper clips as necessary.

4

Place the folded paper on the cutting mat and cut away the surplus paper with the craft knife. Pay particular attention when cutting the small internal areas. It may not be possible to cut through all the layers at once but the pressure of the knife should mark the cutting lines and two or three layers can be cut together.

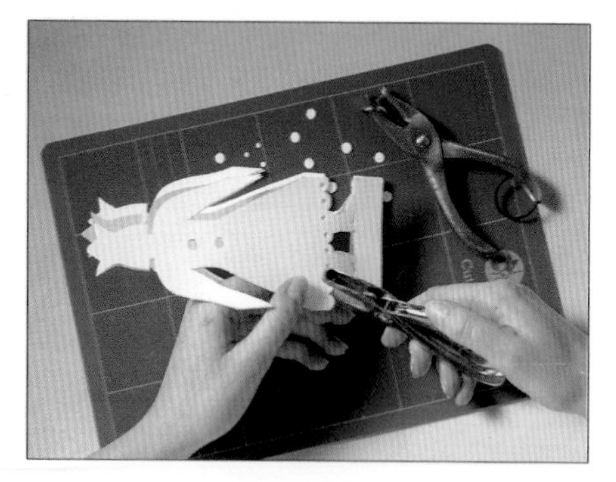

5

When all the layers have been cut use the larger of the hole punchers to make two holes in the bodice of the dress. This will also need to be done in stages, two or three layers at a time. Use the smaller hole punch to make a row of holes in the same manner along the hem of the skirt.

6

Once again working with two or three layers at a time, cut away the slits on the upper sleeves and skirt area. This can be done freehand or the areas to be cut can be marked in pencil first. To ensure that all the slits are cut identically, mark through the first slits onto the paper beneath with a pencil to make guidelines for cutting.

Use these templates at this size.

Three-dimensional Flowers

MOST PEOPLE MUST KNOW OF or even own rather battered examples of these fold-out, three-dimensional decorations. Although the technique has developed into mass produced plastic varieties, it is still easy to find the traditional examples around Christmas-time. They are normally manufactured in the Far East, in countries such as Taiwan, and the favoured material is tissue or very thin paper. Consequently they are a little fragile.

These striking examples in the form of large open flowers are made from the more durable duotone crepe paper. This has the magical effect of showing a different colour on the opposite side of the sheet, a quality has been exploited to make the flower centre and petals tonally contrasting. This emphasises the design brilliantly and has the added effect of having the opposite colour combination on the reverse, best seen when the flower is suspended from the ceiling, perhaps with paperchains made from the same duotone paper.

MATERIALS

- Duotone crepe paper (here in lilac/mauve, yellow/orange and red/pink combinations)
- Template (see page 95)
- Paper clips
- Scissors
- White glue
- Flat-ended modelling tool
- Two strips of deep orange card 2 x 27 cm (3/4 x 10 3/4 in)
- Hole puncher
- Red string or twisted paper cord

1

Pleat the crepe paper concertina-style into rectangles slightly larger than the template and about eight layers thick. Hold the template in place with the paper clips and cut around the shape with the scissors. Repeat until you have 50 separate pieces of crepe paper.

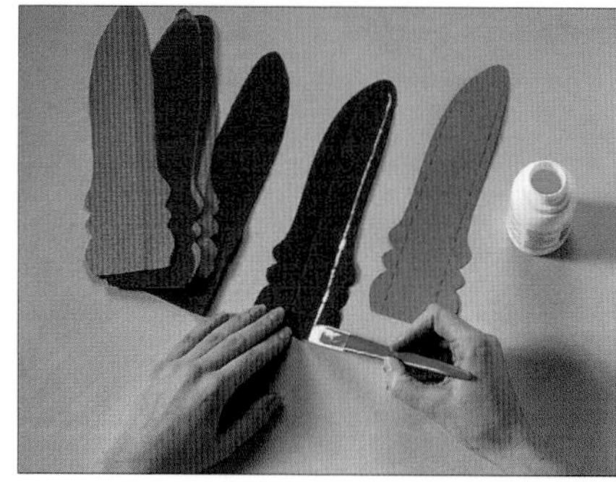

2

Lay the petals down on the table and glue, using the flat ended tool, down the straight side as shown. The gluing line is marked by a dotted line on the template. It is important that the glue is applied in a thin line and that it doesn't spread onto the scalloped section at the base of the petal. Lay a corresponding petal onto the glued one making sure that the same colours are facing, in this case the deep orange.

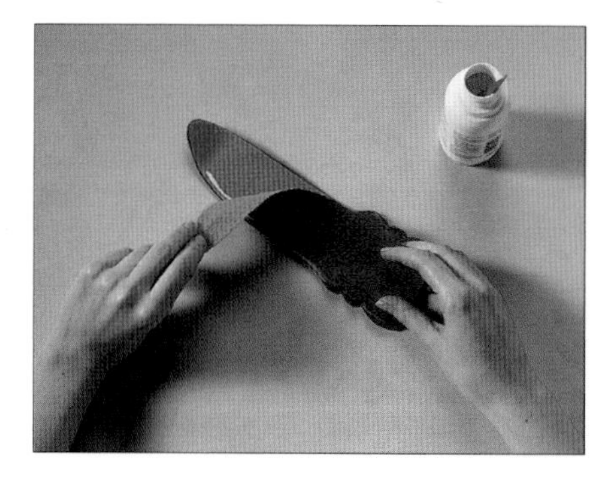

3

This leaves you with a yellow petal uppermost. Apply the glue in the same way along the opposite, curved side of the yellow petal, stopping before the tip as indicated by the dotted line on the template.

4

Continue sticking in this manner until approximately 50 petals are joined. Allow the glue to dry thoroughly. Turn the paper so that the deep orange side of main petal faces you and carefully make the central part of the flower by sticking each of the free scalloped sections together. On this side of the flower you will stick the deep orange sides together so that the yellow sides will show outwardly. You must take great care to put just the smallest dab of glue onto the very tips of these scallops.

5

Allow the glue to dry thoroughly and turn the flower over and repeat the same process on the other side, this time with the yellow sides together so that the deep orange side will show outwardly.

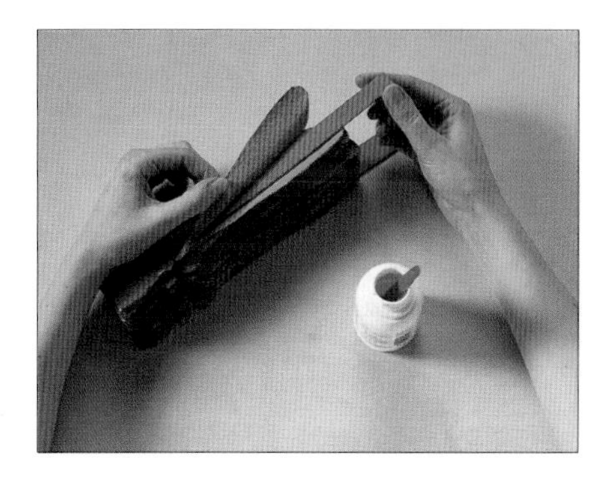

6

Dab some glue onto one side of the card strip and stick onto the last petal on one end. Slot the other piece of card between the last two petals on the other side. Allow the glue to dry.

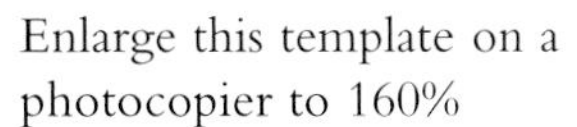

Enlarge this template on a photocopier to 160%

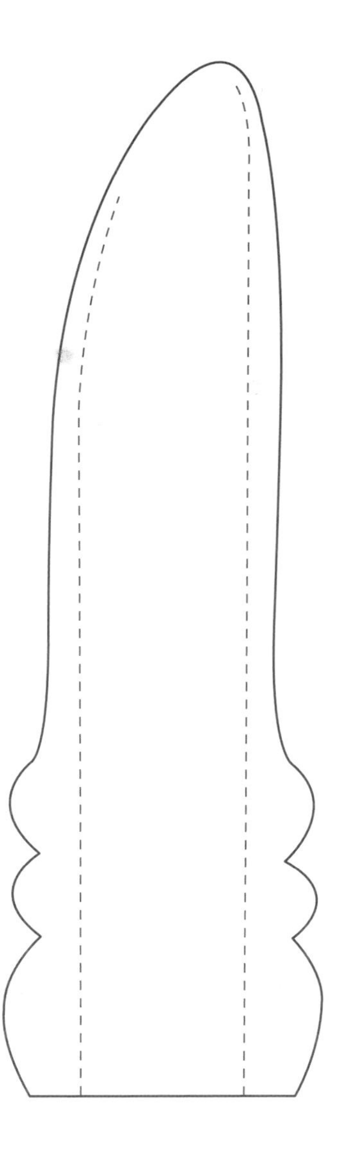

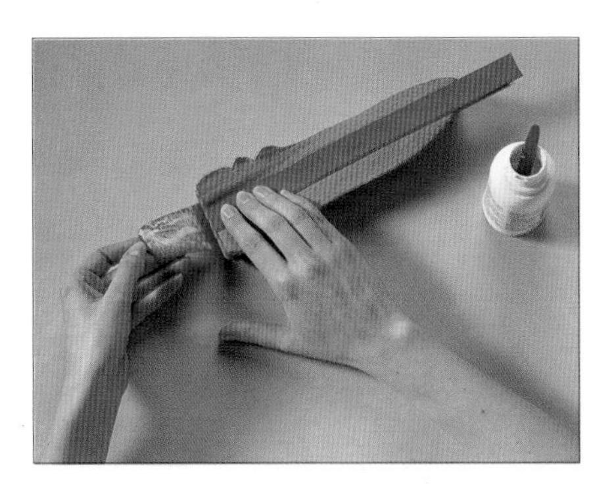

7

Cut a piece of crepe paper long enough to go around the base of the glued petals and reach 4 cm (1½ in) up each side. Cut the ends round and stick in place as shown. You need to be quite generous with the glue in order to hold the petals firmly all together at the base. Allow the glue to dry thoroughly.

8

Punch a hole at the end of each card strip. Holding the card strips at each end, open out the flower until the card strips are touching. Thread a length of matching string through the punched holes and tie together to keep the flower open. The string can also be used to suspend the flower, if you wish.

Christmas Gift Baskets

THE CRAFT OF BASKET-MAKING is one of the most ancient and universal activities. Primarily made as purely functional objects, the materials, weaving patterns and eventual shape of the baskets mean that they are some of the most beautiful examples of human creativity and ingenuity.

These little festive woven gift baskets employ the simplest of basket-making techniques and are very easy to make once you have mastered the method of construction. They cost virtually nothing to create as scraps of paper are used. The ones pictured here have been woven from strips of recycled paper and French Toile de Jouy wallpaper, but any combination can be used. The wonderful thing about weaving is that the method of construction influences the final colour and pattern of the basket. Use colours to match your Christmas theme and fill the baskets with enticing edible gifts.

MATERIALS

Scrap paper (here sand-coloured soft cotton rag paper and patterned wallpaper were used)

Small stapler

White glue

Small scissors

Paper clips

Mattress needle or needle with wide eye

Paper cord

Pinking shears

Two clothes pegs

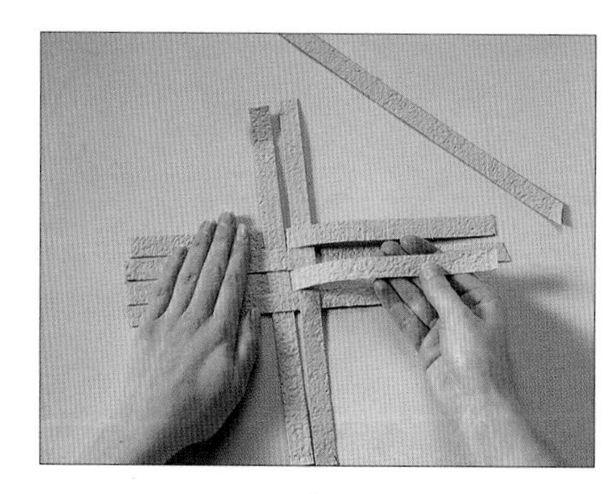

1

Cut seven strips of the plain paper, each approximately 30 cm (12 in) long and 2 cm (¾ in) wide. Lay them down on the worksurface and weave together as shown, laying three strips across four to form the rectangular base of the basket.

2

Use the stapler to staple each of the four corners in order to hold the base firmly in place before building up the sides.

6

Cut a length of the plain paper 2 cm (¾ in) wide and long enough to go around the rim of the basket with a small overlap. Fold it in half lengthways and fit over the rim as shown, holding temporarily in place with paper clips.

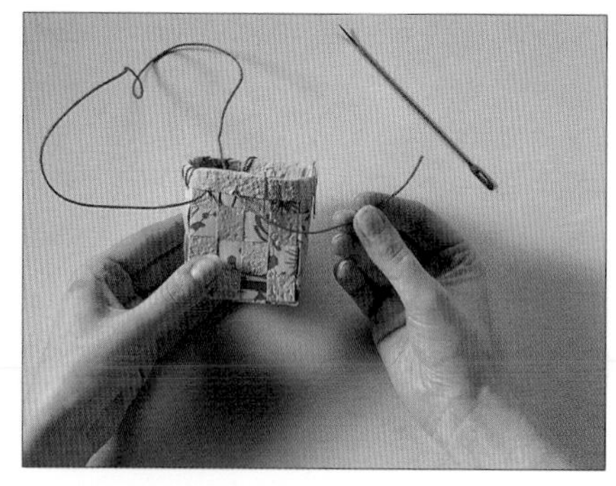

7

Use the needle to pierce holes in the woven section of the basket just below the rim and thread the paper cord through and over the rim. Finish off neatly and stick the end of the cord inside with white glue to secure.

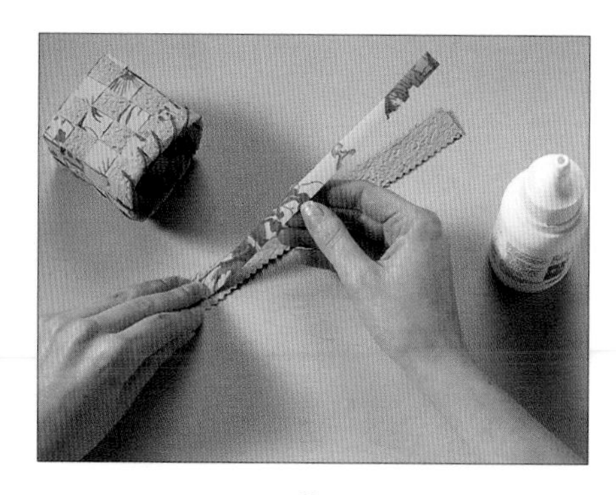

8

Cut a strip of the plain paper 2 cm (¾ in) wide and 22 cm (8½ in) long. Cut each side with the pinking shears to make a pretty zigzagged edge. Stick a strip of the patterned paper 1 cm (½ in) wide along the centre to make the handle.

3

Bend up all the strips to create the basic structure of the basket. Cut lengths from the patterned wallpaper with the same measurements as before and weave the first layer alternately over and under the upright strips, gluing the beginning and end of each horizontal strip to hold it in place.

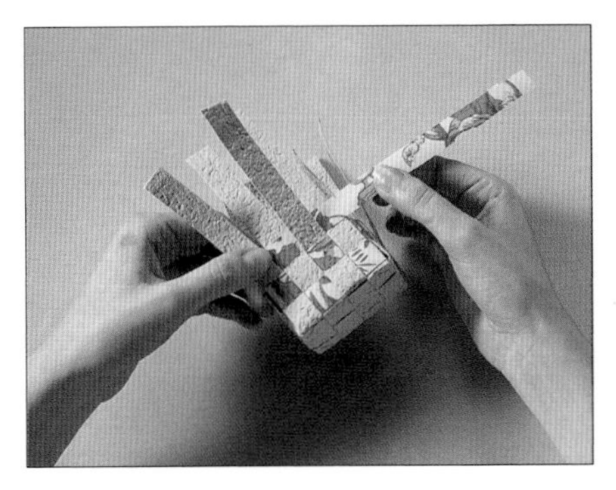

4

Continue weaving in the patterned paper, making sure all the corners form neat right angles. Gently bend the paper here to help it hold the shape of the basket.

5

Continue weaving until four layers are in place, then cut off the excess vertical strips using the small scissors.

9

Glue each end inside the basket and hold in place with clothes pegs until the glue is completely dry and the handle firmly attached.

Gifts

The greetings card market is enormous and mass-produced products are relatively expensive. How much nicer it is to receive a card or gift that has been especially made with you in mind and how fulfilling to be the artist who makes it. Paper has such an enduring quality and antique decorative items are highly sought after and collected as treasured possessions.

Change of Address Card

THERE IS SOMETHING STARKLY beautiful about the crisp white effect of undecorated card. Even when you write the details of your change of address across the front of the house it will not really alter the bold simplicity of this original design. If you really wish to preserve the purity of the white card, simply write your new address on the back.

The techniques of cutting and folding used to make the house stand up without any additional support mean that your new address will not be mislaid by its recipients as it will serve as a striking mantelpiece or kitchen shelf decoration for some time after its receipt. The symmetrical shape of the English-style dolls' house with its accompanying trees at either side is very satisfying.

MATERIALS

Thin card, ivory 300 gsm

Template (see page 104)

Paper clips

Fine pen

Cutting mat

Craft knife

Metal ruler

Scoring tool (a knitting needle or blunt knife will suffice)

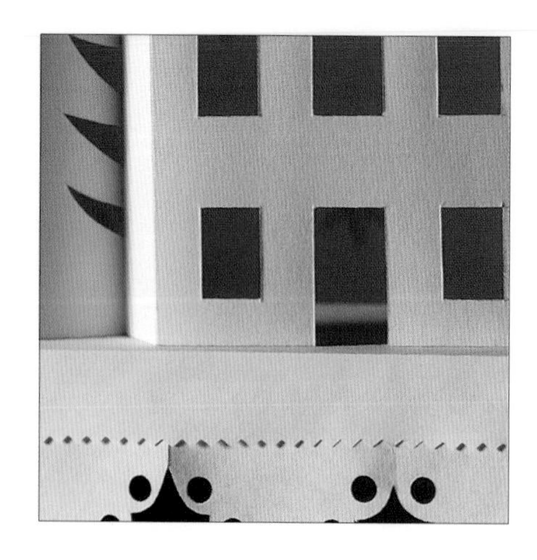

1

Secure the template with the paper clips to a piece of ivory card which has been cut so that it is slightly larger than the actual template. Draw around the template with a fine pen.

2

Place the card on a cutting mat and carefully cut around the marked lines with the craft knife and a metal ruler.

3

Turn the house over to the right side and score the lines that fold back using the knitting needle and the metal ruler (i.e. the middle of the trees, where the house front and sides meet and where the house front meets the roof).

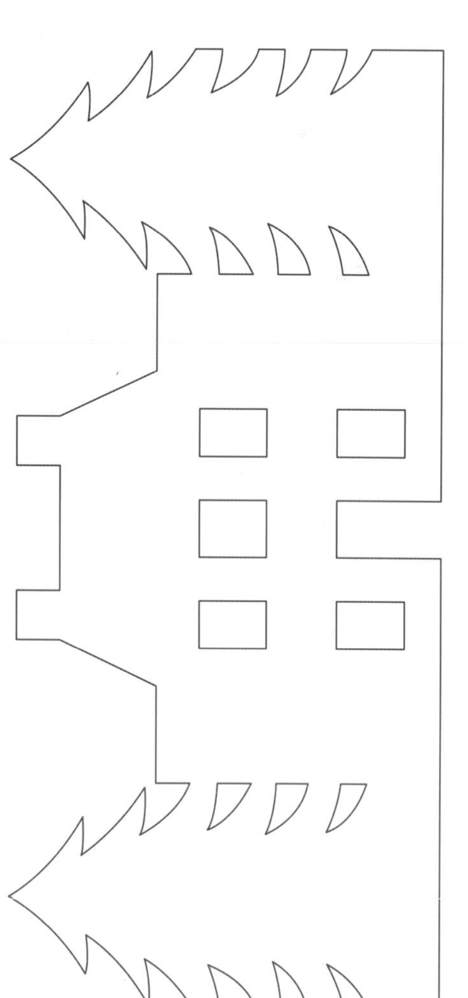

4

Now turn the house over to the back again and score the lines which will fold forward from the front (i.e. where the house meets the tree and between the roof and the chimney pots).

5

Turn the house over again so that the right side is facing you and bend the scored lines backwards or forwards to create the three-dimensional effect which enables the card to stand independently. You can now write your change of address along the front of the house and up the trees on either side.

Enlarge this template on a photocopier to 236%

Gift Tags

THESE SUBTLE AND ELEGANT glove-shaped gift tags have been inspired by American folk art designs from the mid-nineteenth century. The heart was a favourite image and although it was presented as a traditional Valentine, it was also used as an image to symbolize enduring friendship. The hand or glove design is extremely apt to use as a gift tag due to its connotations of friendship and generosity.

The clever interlocking method used in this project to attach the heart to the back of the glove is deceptively simple and could be developed to produce a more intricate and decorative pattern. It is both pretty and extremely functional as no glue is needed. The use of hand-made and recycled paper gives the tags a natural, understated quality. Plant paper was used to wrap the gifts to create a restrained effect.

One inventive aspect of this project is the use of tracing wheels to create the raised bobbly or punctured lines that decorate the gloves so effectively. These are readily available from haberdashery departments and can be adapted to all sorts of decorative applications.

MATERIALS

- Templates (see page 111)
- Hand-made ivory paper
- Paper clips
- Pencil
- Small pointed scissors
- Recycled pink paper
- Pinking shears
- Wad of tissue paper
- Tracing wheel (in two sizes)
- Craft knife
- Cutting mat
- Rubber
- White glue
- Length of ribbon
- Hole puncher

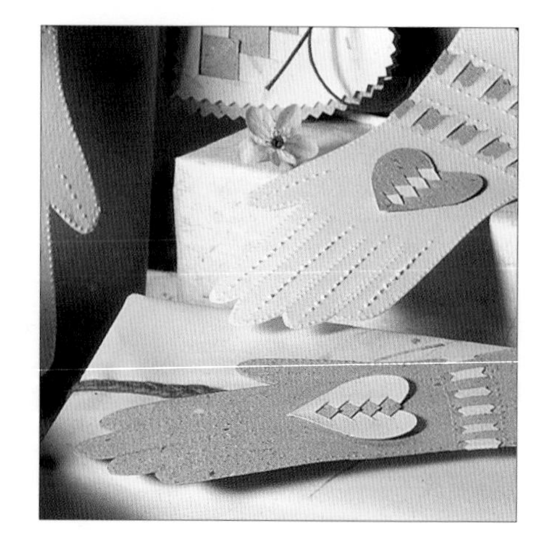

1

Place the template on the ivory coloured paper and hold in place with paper clips. Draw around it with the pencil, remove the template and cut around the glove shape with the small scissors.

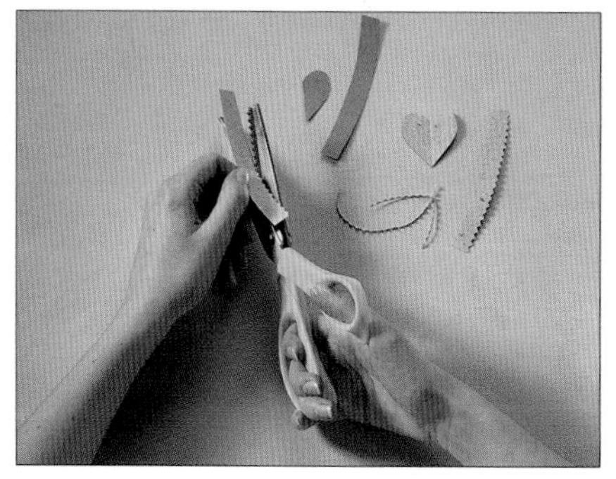

2

Fold the pink paper in half and place the straight side of the heart template against the fold. Cut out the heart plus the two curved strips, also using the template provided. Cut a zigzagged edge with the pinking shears along each edge of the strips.

3

Place the glove shape on a wad of tissue paper to act as a yielding surface. Using the smaller tracing wheel, press firmly whilst wheeling it all around the edge of the glove. Make two parallel lines between each finger.

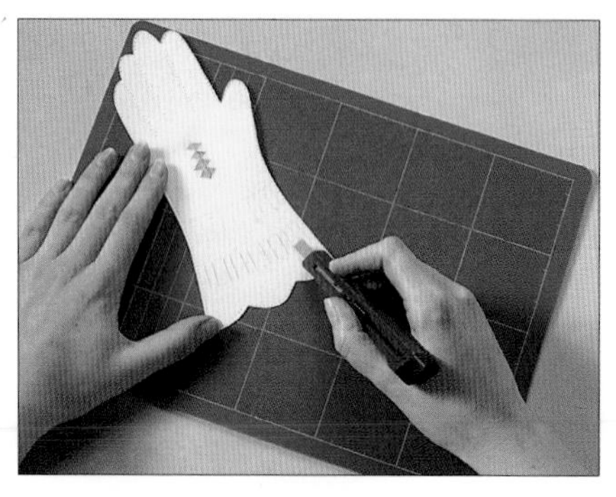

6

Place the curved template onto the cuff of the back of the glove and draw two sets of parallel lines. Place the glove onto the cutting mat and cut 12 slits on the outer band between these lines and ten slits on the inner one.

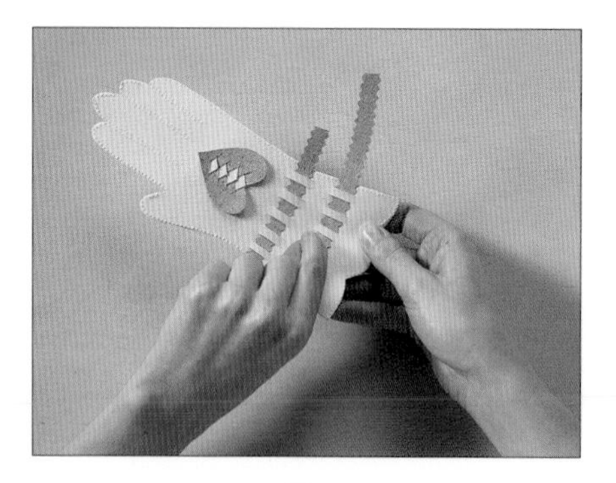

7

Turn the glove over to the right side and slot the pinked strips through the slits. Trim the ends so that 1 cm (½ in) overlaps, turn under to the back of the glove and stick down with paper glue.

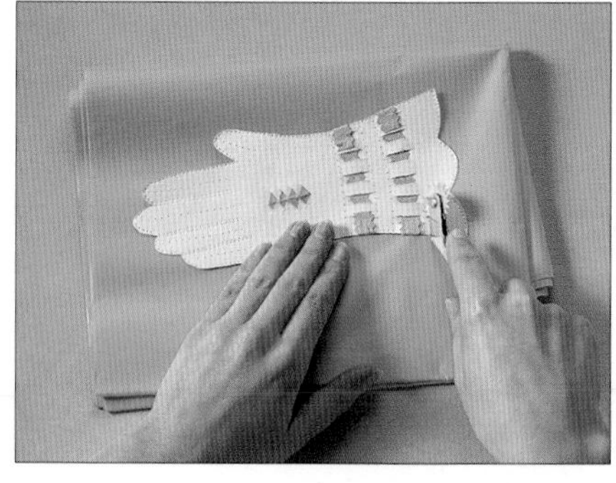

8

Still working from the wrong side, place the glove on the tissue paper and using the larger tracing wheel, mark each side of the strips on the cuff and along the centre of each finger and the thumb. To attach a ribbon, punch a hole at the edge of the cuff.

4

Open up the pink heart, lay it on the glove with the point facing the cuff end. Lightly draw around with a sharp pencil. Now cut four parallel v-shaped slits into the heart and in the heart shape on the back of the glove. Each arm of the slits should measure 1 cm (½ in).

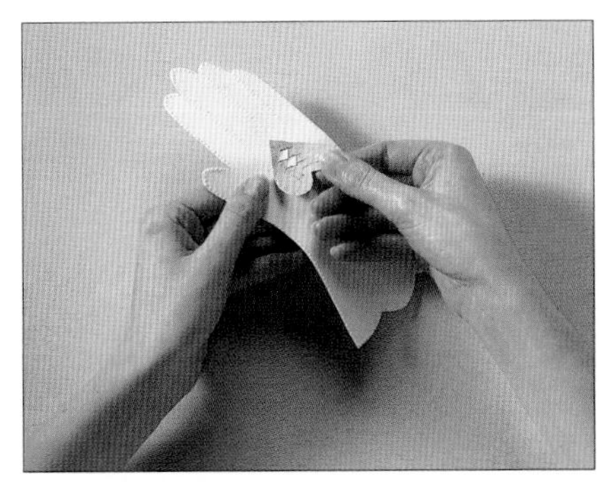

5

Rub out the pencil marks on the glove. Take the heart, now with its pointed end facing the fingers, and carefully interlock the points of the corresponding slits. The heart is now securely fixed onto the glove.

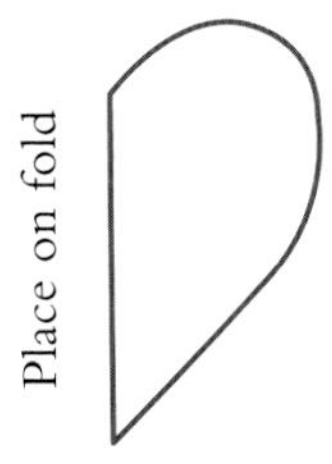

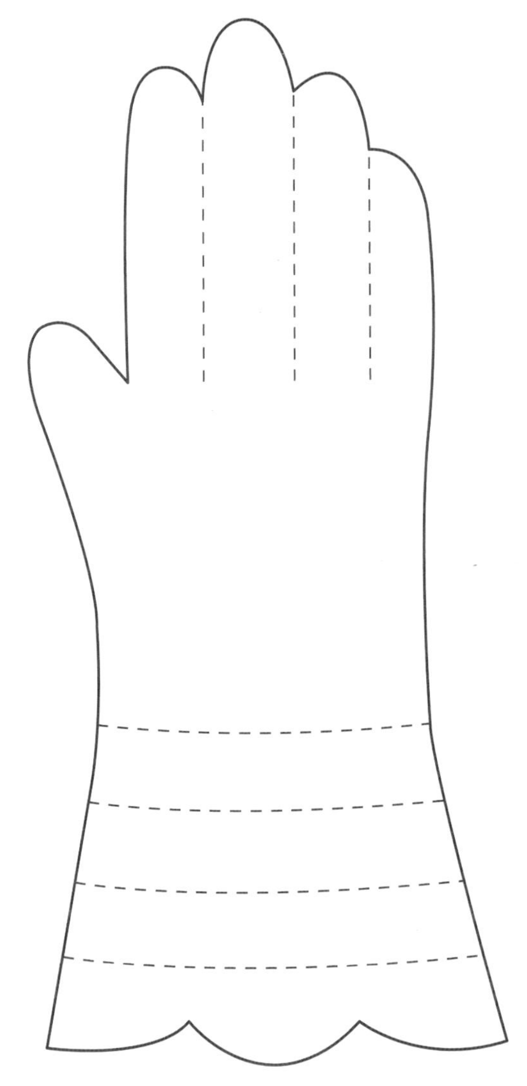

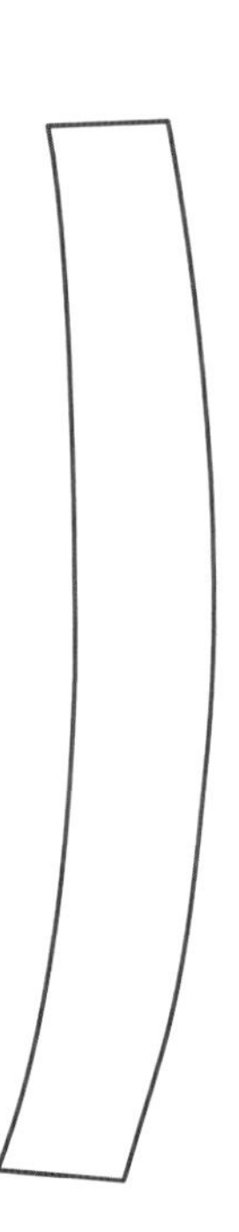

Enlarge these templates on a photocopier to 137%

Photo Album

As a photograph album contains treasured memories of family, friends and special occasions, it seems worthwhile making it really personal by creating your own papercut cover design.

You will need only the smallest amount of collected scrap paper, wallpaper, unusual hand-painted wrapping paper and small scraps to create this book cover. It is a combination of bold and intricate design. Everyone is familiar with the well known technique of making papercut snowflakes from their early childhood and the simple, stylized plant in the pot is inspired by central European papercutting traditions.

The small range of purples and subtly related colours has to some extent been dictated by the original colour of the undecorated book. Once you become familiar with the different techniques and traditions in this craft, it is much easier to adapt and combine them to make new and interesting designs to suit your own needs.

MATERIALS

- Ready made photo album, 32 cm (12 ½ in) square
- Templates (see page 114-115)
- Pencil
- Paper clips
- Pale striped wallpaper
- Poster paper in violet and purple
- Hand-painted wrapping paper
- Small pointed scissors
- White glue
- Cotton bud
- Hole puncher
- Pinking shears

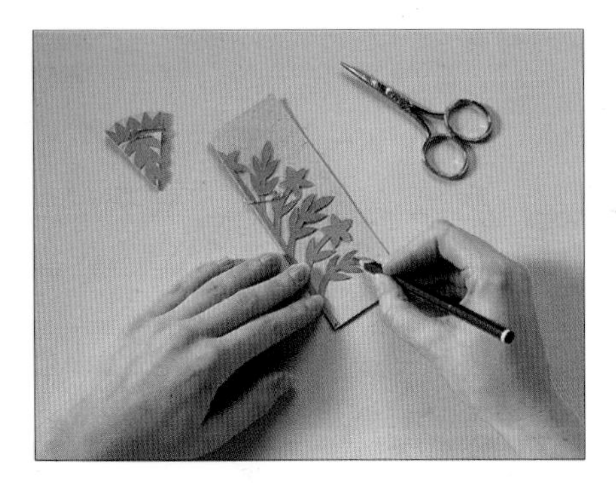

1

Fold a piece of the striped wallpaper in half and place the straight edge of the plant template against the fold. Secure with paper clips and draw around it with the pencil. Cut a circle 12 cm (4¾ in) in diameter also from the wallpaper and fold into eight (see page 42 for folding instructions). Attach the snowflake template with paper clips and draw around it with the pencil.

2

Use the small pointed scissors to cut out the plant and the snowflake. When cutting out intricate shapes, it helps to turn the paper rather than the scissors.

3

Cut out a rectangle of the violet poster paper 10 x 17.5 cm (4 x 6¾ in) and a piece of the purple 10.5 cm (4¼ in) square. Glue the snowflake and the plant motif carefully in place onto their respective backgrounds. Take care not to get any excess glue on the plain coloured background - it is easiest to pour a little glue onto a scrap of paper and then apply it with a cotton bud.

4

Cut a thin tapering strip from the hand-painted paper and stick along the main stem. Punch out five dots from the same paper and stick in place in the centre of each flower. Cut a pot from the striped wallpaper with pinking shears, making sure that the stripes go horizontally and stick in place over the base of the plant stem.

5

Cut two strips from the hand-painted patterned paper, one 3.5 x 29 cm (1½ x 11¾ in) and the other 5.5 x 29 cm (2¼ x 11¾ in). Stick the thinner strip on the left of the album cover, leave 1 cm (½ in) gap and stick the snowflake square at the top. Leave another 1 cm (½ in) gap and stick the wider strip in place on the right. Finally, stick the rectangle with the plant in the remaining space, leaving even borders all around.

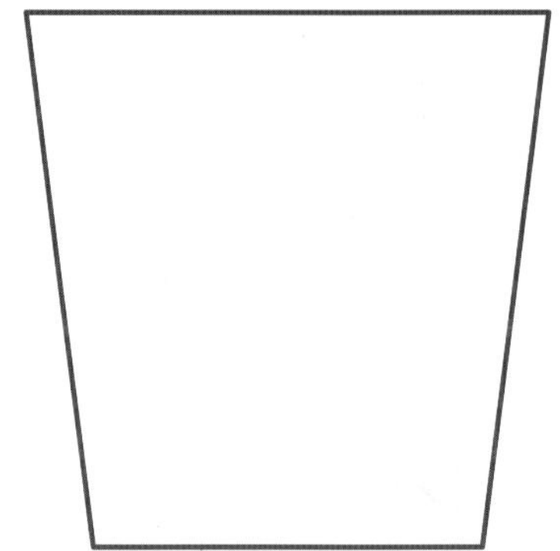

Enlarge these templates on a photocopier to 117%

Alphabet Cubes

THESE ALPHABET CUBES are not difficult to make providing you take great care to be accurate, both with the cutting and with the folding. More contemporary in feel than some of the other projects in this book, they have both a practical and decorative use.

The letters have been made by enlarging different type faces on a photocopier to the same size. They have then been carefully drawn onto three faces of the cubes before being cut out. Although A, B and C are provided on the accompanying template, you can easily create your own letters to complete the alphabet. The important thing to remember is to design the letters with little strips of card remaining between the curves of the letters, thus ensuring the cut pieces of card do not fall out where they are not intended to.

Because the cubes are lightweight and therefore easy to handle, a young child can use them as toys in the form of building blocks and have the added bonus of becoming familiar with the form and shapes of the letters in the process.

MATERIALS

Template (see page 120)

Coverboard, 300 gsm, in shades of blue and green

Fine pen

Craft knife

Cutting mat

Scissors

Knitting needle or scoring tool

Metal ruler

Double-sided tape

Enlarge this template on a photocopier to 181%

1

Lay the template onto the blue card, hold firmly with one hand and carefully draw around the outer edges and the inside of the letter shapes with the pen.

2

Cut around the outer edges of the template, then place the card on the cutting mat and cut away the outside and inside the letter shapes using the craft knife. Take particular care when cutting around the curved sides of the letters.

3

Use the knitting needle and the metal ruler to score the lines indicated on the template between the separate sides and along the sides with the tabs. You will need to press firmly.

4

Stick the double-sided tape along the tabs as shown and neatly cut off any excess at the angled ends with the scissors or craft knife.

5

Bend along the scored lines between the separate sides and bend each tab over at right angles.

6

Pull off the protective layer on the tape and very carefully and accurately stick the tab to its corresponding side. Press the metal ruler along the inside of the join to make it stick firmly. The last side is more difficult to stick and you will need to press the ruler along these last joins by pushing it carefully through the cut away letters.

Butterfly Greetings Cards

THE SYMMETRICAL FORM of the butterfly lends itself beautifully to papercutting techniques. The template for this project was designed by drawing one half of a butterfly form onto a piece of folded paper, cutting out that side, opening up the fold and revealing the perfect symmetrical shape. In this way you can design a host of different butterfly shapes to use as card decorations. The glittery backing which has been pasted onto the reverse side of the butterfly enhances the design as well as making a particular eye-catching effect.

Once you have made the card shown with the template provided, stretch your imagination and design more symmetrical motifs that would work in the same way as the butterfly. A heart is an obvious one or try a vase of flowers or a cat's face. This is an ideal project to involve children in.

MATERIALS

- Coverboard, china white, 300 gsm
- Template (see page 125)
- Paper clips
- Fine pen
- Small scissors
- Craft knife
- Cutting mat
- Hole puncher
- Metallic paper in pink, orange, blue, red and green
- White glue
- Aerosol glue (optional)
- Coverboard, 300 gsm, for mounting in blue, green, orange and pink
- Pinking shears

1

Attach the butterfly template to the ivory paper with paper clips and draw around it carefully using the fine pen.

2

Remove the template and cut around the butterfly shape using the small scissors. Cut away the internal sections with the craft knife working on the cutting mat. Cut carefully around the larger circles on the wing but leave the smaller ones uncut.

3

Using the hole puncher, carefully make the holes around the larger circles on the wings.

6

Lay the butterfly down on the cutting mat and score vertical lines either side of the body using the knitting needle.

7

Fold the wings forward along the two scored lines and curve slightly. Curl the two antennae in the same manner.

8

Cut a 13 x 17 cm (5 x 6¾ in) piece of orange coverboard and fold in half. Stick the butterfly's body onto the front of the card.

4

Cut a piece of the pink metallic paper and stick the butterfly onto this paper, making sure the thin layer of glue covers the back of the butterfly. Be careful not to let any glue ooze onto the metallic paper underneath. If you are familiar with aerosol glue use this, but be sure to follow all safety regulations.

5

When the glue has dried cut around the butterfly with the pinking shears leaving a pretty zigzagged edge showing. Take particular care when cutting around the antennae.

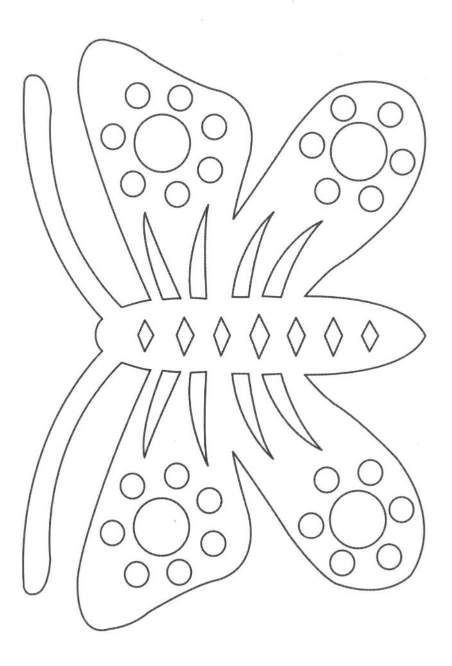

Enlarge this template on a photocopier to 205%

Valentine Picture (see pages 70-73)
Use these templates at this size.

Star Light (see pages 46–49)

Enlarge this template on a photocopier to 191%

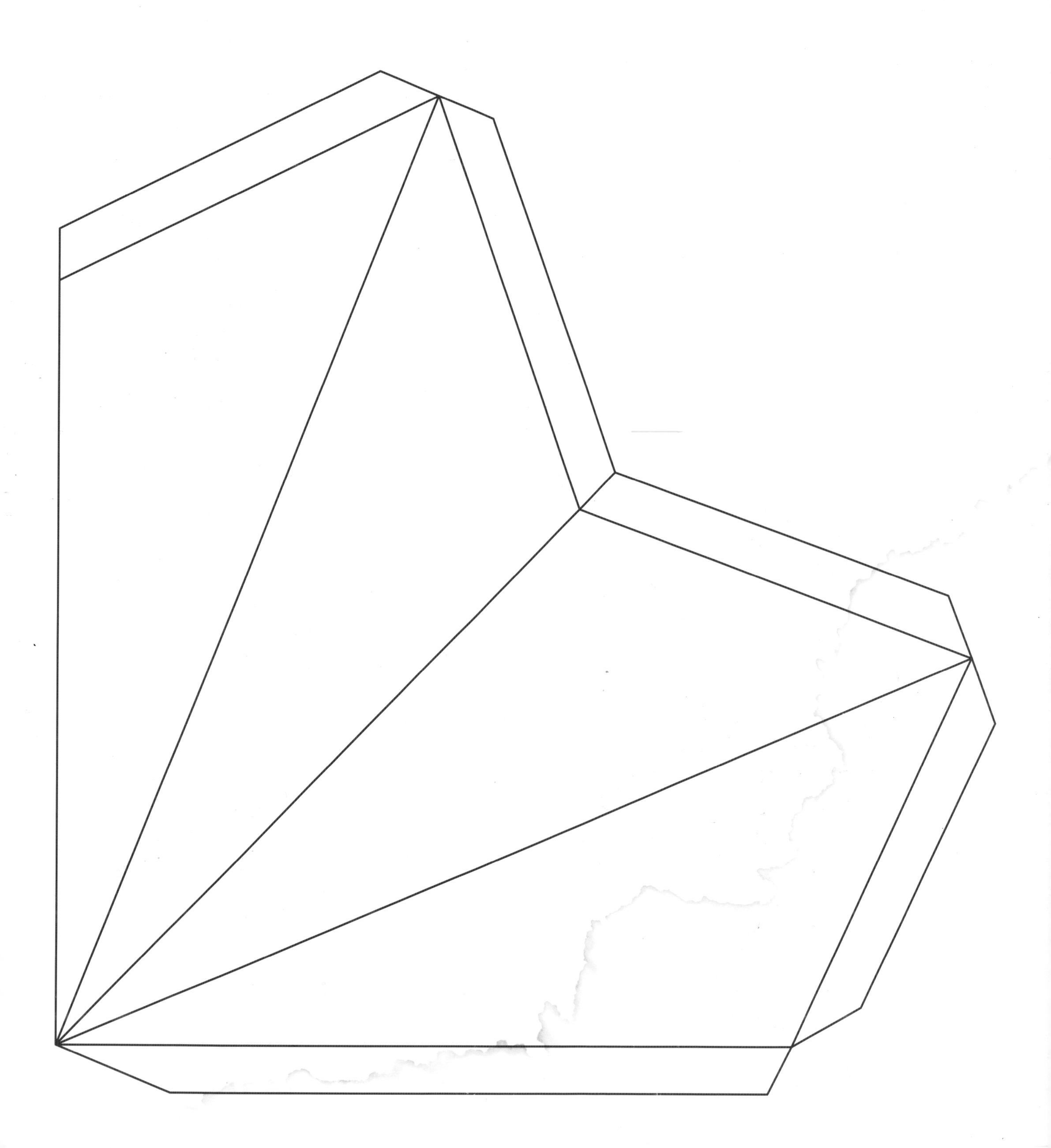

INDEX